MARANDA'S GUIDE TO FAMILY FUN IN WEST MICHIGAN

MARY BETH BARKELEY AND KATHY MULLEN

WILLIAM B. EERDMANS PUBLISHING COMPANY
GRAND RAPIDS, MICHIGAN

Maranda hosts WXMI Fox 17's **Kids Club** and **Fox Pause,** and frequently appears in communities all over West Michigan.

Parents and families often ask about her travels and for information about various events. They also ask where the events are located, and what age groups they attract. **Maranda's Guide to Family Fun in West Michigan** was written to answer these questions, and to assist families in planning their time together.

MARY BETH BARKELEY and KATHY MULLEN live in Grand Rapids and are actively involved in community and school volunteer work. Mary Beth, the mother of three children, serves as a fund-raiser for the Retinitis Pigmentosa Foundation and teaches Sunday school. Kathy, the mother of four children, is a free-lance writer who serves as a trustee for the Specific Language Disability Center and as a Science Olympiad coach. They and their families are constantly searching for creative and fun things to do and treasure their many adventures (and misadventures) in West Michigan.

Left to right: Maranda, Mary Beth Barkeley, Kathy Mullen.

Copyright © 1994 by Wm. B. Eerdmans Publishing Co.
255 Jefferson Ave. S.E., Grand Rapids, Michigan 49503

Printed in the United States of America

00 99 98 97 96 95 94   7 6 5 4 3 2 1

Library of Congress Cataloging-in-Publication Data

Barkeley, Mary Beth, 1962-
    Maranda's guide to family fun in west Michigan / Mary Beth Barkeley
    and Kathy Mullen.
        p.   cm.
    Includes index.
    ISBN 0-8028-7058-9
    1. Family recreation — Michigan — Directories.
    I. Mullen, Kathy, 1955-   . II. Title.
    GV182.8.B37   1994
    790.1′91′09774 — dc20   94-24396
                                                      CIP

CONTENTS

INTRODUCTION

I am very pleased to present *Maranda's Guide to Family Fun in West Michigan* to you. My hope is that you and your children will enjoy many hours of entertainment and fun together, and learn some new things, too! I also hope that every adventure leaves you feeling great about West Michigan. Most importantly, though, take a moment to appreciate how lucky you are to have a family with whom to share all these special experiences.

A portion of the proceeds from the sales of this book will be donated to charity. Fox 17 and Eerdmans Publishing Company will contribute to a charity that improves the quality of life for children and families in West Michigan. As the exclusive sponsor of *Maranda's Guide to Family Fun in West Michigan,* D&W Food Centers will make a contribution to the Kent County Literacy Council. By purchasing this book, you are helping kids in our communities achieve their dreams.

I would like to thank our two authors, Mary Beth Barkeley and Kathy Mullen, for their hard work and mountainous efforts.

Details and descriptions were accurate as this book went to print, but Murphy's Law guarantees that changes will occur. Please be sure to call ahead to confirm all information!

Thanks for your support. ENJOY!

—Maranda

viii

ART • THEATER • MUSIC

1

Art

Battle Creek

Art Center of Battle Creek

The Art Center offers classes and workshops in all artistic mediums, and exhibits change frequently.

The "Kidspace" Gallery, organized in conjunction with two professional exhibitions during the school year, features hands-on activities and fun in a variety of mediums, all to get children's creative juices flowing. Call for specific dates.

Both children and adults will love the handcrafted work by Michigan artists in the Art Center's Michigan Artworks Shop. Prints, paintings, ceramics, and much more are offered in all price ranges; the jewelry is especially notable.

Dates/Hours:	Tuesday–Friday 10–5, Saturday–Sunday 1–4
Admission:	Free; donations welcome
Phone:	962-9511
Address:	265 E. Emmett

3

Grand Rapids

Passageways Gallery

Located in the Grand Rapids Art Museum's lower level, the small Passageways Gallery offers hands-on exhibits that almost beg for a child's touch.

Older kids may also enjoy the main-level exhibits, including six centuries of art in traveling exhibitions and a growing permanent collection.

Dates/Hours: Tuesday/Sunday 12–4,
                          Wednesday/Friday/Saturday 10–4,
                          Thursday 10–9,
                          closed Monday
Admission: Adults $2; students $.50;
                          5 and under free
Phone: 459-4676
Address: 155 N. Division, downtown Grand Rapids

Grand Rapids

Peace Education Week at Breton Village

Art

Grand Rapids area schoolchildren display their considerable artistic ability in paintings, sculptures, and multimedia works each year during Peace Education Week.

Showcased at Breton Village Mall in southeast Grand Rapids, the art centers around peace and the kind of world children want to live in. Children of all ages will love checking out their peers' work. On Saturday of Peace Education Week, the mall holds many participatory events for kids.

The annual program is cosponsored by the Institute for Global Education and Educators for Social Responsibility.

Dates/Hours:	Third week in February during mall hours; Saturday activities 10 A.M.–2 P.M.
Admission:	Free
Phone:	454-1642, Institute for Global Education
Address:	Breton Village Mall, corner of Burton Street SE and Breton Road

Grand Rapids

Ryerson Gallery

The Grand Rapids Public Library's contribution to art enrichment features revolving displays, such as pictorial accounts of World War II, baseball, and prominent women in Grand Rapids' history. Junior and senior high students will appreciate the informational aspects of these displays.

Gallery photographs are often borrowed from the Public Library's Robinson Collection, which contains over one million photographs.

Dates/Hours:	Daily 9–5:30, Monday–Wednesday 9–9
Admission:	Free
Phone:	456-3622
Address:	60 Library NE, downtown Grand Rapids

Holland

Holland Area Arts Council

Unique to Holland, the Arts Council is a leader in providing arts enrichment for children and adults. The strong education department offers over 40 creative writing, dance, music, and visual arts classes each year. It also includes rotating exhibits and hands-on displays.

"First Friday," aimed at 6–11 year olds, allows children to try out new activities, emphasizing visual arts and centered around a monthly theme. Every other month's First Friday includes "Take Off," where children work on improvisation, theater games, creative music, and play production. Approximately 200 children attend each month!

The Arts Council offers a Creative Arts Camp and Performing Arts Series to encourage arts participation. The gift shop sells educational toys and games; proceeds go to arts programs.

Dates/Hours: Monday–Friday 10–9, Saturday 10–4
               First Friday: First Friday of each month,
               5:00–6:30 P.M.
Admission: Depends on choice of program
Phone: 396-3278
Address: 25 W. 8th Street, downtown Holland

Kalamazoo

Kalamazoo Institute of Arts

A permanent collection of 3,000 objects with emphasis on 20th-century American art is housed in Kalamazoo Institute of Art's award-winning building. In 20 exhibits annually, KIA showcases local talent and exposes the community to international artists from all periods of history.

KIA enrolls over 1,300 children and adults each year in such classes as ceramics, drawing, jewelry, photography, and weaving.

Special programs include Artreach (a traveling exhibition that visits schools and other organizations), Classes with Special Emphasis (for the disabled), ARTist (5th-graders visit KIA for a day), and the Juried High School Show in June. The KIA library has a full range of art reference materials, and the institute also runs a gallery shop and an art rental program.

Dates/Hours: Tuesday–Saturday 10–5, Sunday 1–5
Admission: Free; donations welcome
Phone: 349-7775
Address: 314 S. Park Street, downtown Kalamazoo

Muskegon

Muskegon Museum of Art

Although the Muskegon Museum of Art is not specifically a kids' place, families will enjoy the Annual Student Art Exhibit, featuring works from the Muskegon area's many talented student artists.

The exhibit, sponsored by the Muskegon Area Intermediate School District and the Museum, includes paintings, drawings, masks, sculpture, mixed media, and videos.

The Muskegon Museum of Art is one of the best in the nation for its relatively small size. Its grand and beautiful interior was recently updated with white marble and dramatic wall colors, which accent an impressive collection of paintings and artifacts. The gift shop has a nice selection of prints, books, toys, games, and jewelry.

Dates/Hours: Student Art Exhibit:
               mid-March – May 1
               Hours: Tuesday–Friday 10–5,
               Saturday–Sunday 12–5
Admission: Free; donations accepted
Phone: 722-2600
Address: Bus. U.S. 31, north on Third to Webster
               Avenue, one block east of Hackley Park,
               Muskegon

ART • THEATER • MUSIC

Theater

Battle Creek

United Arts Council

The Battle Creek United Arts Council is responsible for Family Place and Discovery Theatre.

Family Place presents two educational themes each year, and plans children's hands-on exhibits accordingly. Music might be one main theme, for example. Fantasy Forest is an annual display that uses lighted characters to depict Christmas in other countries (Santa and hot chocolate make this one extra fun).

BCUAC's Discovery Theatre sponsors performances by various entertainers. Call to find out if your children might enjoy one.

The organization's Family Series is a set of four annual family shows.

Dates/Hours: Varies
Admission: Discovery theatre: Adults $6; students
$3. Season passes available
Phone: 962-5752
Address: Family Place: 17 W. Michigan. Discovery
Theatre: 51 W. Michigan, Battle Creek

11

Theater

Grand Haven

Grand Theatre

Some things never change. This historic mainstreet theater offers current movie releases at an old-fashioned $.99 per ticket.

Dates/Hours: April 1–October, all shows
Admission: $.99
Phone: 842-4520
Address: 22 Washington, Grand Haven

Grand Rapids

Civic Children's Theatre

The enormously popular Civic Children's Theatre produces two plays each year, and offers acting classes for kids 8 years to adult. One popular past Children's Theatre production was *The Velveteen Rabbit*.

The Civic Theatre is comprised of many dedicated local actors, and is one of the oldest and largest community theaters in the country. It holds six major stage productions per year.

Dates/Hours: Call for performance schedules
Admission: $2–$9.50
Phone: 456-9301
Address: 30 N. Division, downtown Grand Rapids

Theater

13

Grand Rapids

Community Circle Theatre in the Park

Circle Theatre's stage productions are held for both children (Magic Circle Theatre) and adults from May to September. See actors in our own community present classics and originals in an intimate theater in the round.

During intermissions, stroll through the rose garden or watch the ducks in the John Ball Park pond. It's a lovely way to spend a summer evening!

Dates/Hours: Call for schedule of performances. Shows usually begin at 8 P.M.
Admission: Varies, usually $15 per ticket
Phone: 456-6656
Address: John Ball Park Pavilion, Fulton Street NW, Grand Rapids

14

Grand Rapids

Family Performing Arts Series

The Council of Performing Arts for Children (CPAC) offers an array of participatory shows geared toward kids. All run less than one hour.

CPAC holds six performances annually.

Dates/Hours: Call for schedule
Admission: Members $3; nonmembers $5
             Memberships are available
Phone: 774-9922
Address: Various locations

15

Theater

Grand Rapids

Grand Rapids Ballet

While the Grand Rapids Ballet stages family-oriented performances — a fall repertory performance, Christmas's
Nutcracker, and a full-length spring production — the organization also has two other major family pleasers: its
Family Series and Junior Company.

The Family Series, held at St. Cecilia Auditorium, is
geared for younger children. The performances are typically based on fairy tales and last about one hour. Tickets
cost $4.50 per person. The Junior Company is made up
of 9–14-year-old ballet students who attend classes and
perform.

The Grand Rapids Ballet also offers classes for all skill
and age levels.

Dates/Hours: Varies by program
Admission: $4.50 per ticket for Family Series
                 Nutcracker tickets: adults $21;
                 students $19
Phone: 454-4771
Address: St. Cecilia Auditorium, DeVos Hall, and
                 Civic Theatre, downtown Grand Rapids

Holland

Children's Performance Troupe

Part of the Hope Summer Repertory Theatre group is the Children's Performance Troupe, which schedules two children's productions, held in the intimate Studio Theatre. Located in DeWitt Center's lower level, Studio Theatre is a theater in the round.

Held for two weeks in August, the two productions alternate between morning and afternoon performances on Mondays, Wednesdays, and Fridays.

Your children might also enjoy the family-oriented shows given by the regular part of the Repertory Theatre. For example, *Music Man* appealed greatly to kids!

Dates/Hours: Call for detailed information
Admission: Children's Performance Troupe:
             $4 per ticket
Phone: 394-7890
Address: Hope College's DeWitt Center, Holland

17

Theater

Kalamazoo

Civic Youth Theatre

Three children's productions, by children and for children, are scheduled each year in Kalamazoo. Your child could be the next Snow White (or a dwarf!), or maybe one of the Three Musketeers!

The Youth Theatre also runs very popular weekly summer classes. Register early to reserve a place. Sessions last six weeks.

Dates/Hours: Varies
Admission: Performances: adults $5.50; children 18 and under $4. Groups of 20+ in advance: $3
Phone: 342-9867
Address: Civic Players Building: 329 S. Park Street, Kalamazoo

Kalamazoo

Junior Ballet Company

This huge ballet company operates a year-round school, drawing students within a 40-mile radius. In addition to its spectacular in-house performances, the Junior Ballet performs in 100 touring shows each year — for a total audience of over 50,000 western Michigan residents.

Classes are offered for all levels and all ages, including a very well-attended summer school.

Dates/Hours:	Varies
Admission:	Varies
Phone:	343-3027
Address:	326 W. Kalamazoo Avenue

Kentwood

Monthly Movie Night

Kids 11 and older will love having their own version of dinner theater, with a movie, pizza, popcorn, and pop, all at the Kentwood Activities Center.

Extra energy can be burned off too — basketball and volleyball are available. Sponsored by the Kentwood Recreation Department.

Dates/Hours:	Varies, on a Friday each month at 6:30 P.M.
Admission:	$3, includes movie and food Pre-registration required
Phone:	531-2391
Address:	355 48th Street SE, Kentwood

Muskegon

Cherry County Playhouse

Eight weeks of plays and musicals every summer feature national and international celebrities (really famous people!). Call for a schedule of performances your children might enjoy.

Pat Paulsen, poker-faced comedian from the old Smothers Brothers Comedy Hour, still stops in to help with production, although he sold his interest in the Playhouse several years ago.

Dates/Hours:	July and August: Tuesday, Wednesday, Friday 8 P.M., Thursday and Saturday 2 P.M. and 8 P.M.
Admission:	Evening $23, matinee $19
Phone:	727-8888
Address:	Bus. U.S 31, Third Street exit. 2 blocks to 411 W. Western Avenue, Muskegon

21

Theater

Dove Foundation Family Film Festival

"Family-friendly" movies are shown free for children 12 and under at Jack Loeks Theatres during the Family Film Festival, held during the eight weeks before Easter and again before Thanksgiving. Past Film Festival titles have included *The Secret Garden, Gettysburg,* and *Beethoven.*

Students may obtain passes from area schools, participating sponsors, and Jack Loeks Theatres.

Also, theaters that display the Dove Foundation seal provide approved feature films. The foundation is currently working to expand the number of participating theater chains.

You may also request a published list of family-friendly videos by calling 554-9993.

Dates/Hours:	Movies dates and times are shown on passes and in newspaper ads
Admission:	Children under 12 free; adults $1
Phone:	554-9993 for list of approved videos and features
Address:	Jack Loeks Theatres are located in Grand Haven, Grand Rapids, Kalamazoo, and Muskegon

Music

Battle Creek

Boychoir

The boys' choir of Battle Creek, made up of the highly talented 7–11 year olds, practices twice each week, and performs about 30 times a year. The boys perform together with the Battle Creek men's choir six times annually.

The Boychoir requires auditions before inviting a boy to join the group. Auditions are held in January and May, and are announced in the *Battle Creek Enquirer*.

Dates/Hours: Practice held twice weekly
Admission: Cost of performances varies substantially
              Monthly tuition is $30–$35
Phone: 963-1911 or 781-7048
Address: Rehearsals: Territorial School
              Performances: Local auditoriums and
              churches

Battle Creek

Youth Orchestra

The Battle Creek Youth Orchestra assists in developing young talent in three stages: Reading Ensemble for early elementary string students, Junior Strings for junior high ages, and Youth Orchestra, a full symphony, for high school ages. These are remarkably talented kids!

The three orchestras perform together four times annually in varied locations; concerts last about 75 minutes. Single tickets cost $8 for adults, $6 for seniors, $4 for students. The best deal, though, is the season tickets at $16 for adults, $8 for seniors, and $8 for students for the group of four performances.

The symphony also sponsors February's Spring Fling Festival for ALL junior high string students, a one-day program of clinics, practices, fun, and an evening performance.

Dates/Hours: Call for information
Admission: Adults $8; seniors $6; children $4
              Season tickets: $16/$12/$8
Phone: 966-2527, Monday and Wednesday
              afternoons
Address: 35 W. Jackson, Battle Creek

24

Battle Creek

Girls' Chorus

The Battle Creek Girls' Chorus was founded in 1987, and is made up of 36 girls ranging from 10 to 15 years of age. The group gives performances around the country and internationally. It was awarded a silver medal at the Toronto International Music Festival in May, 1993.

The Girls' Chorus performs regularly in the Battle Creek area, offering programs from sacred music to Broadway show tunes for a variety of occasions.

Admission to the chorus is by audition, held in January and May. The girls practice every week at Westlake Elementary School. Call 962-6725 for information about booking a performance and for audition details.

Dates/Hours:	Call for performance and practice schedules
Admission:	Cost of performance varies; monthly tuition $30–$35 per child
Phone:	962-6725
Address:	Performances: local auditoriums and churches

Grand Rapids

Choir of Men and Boys

Boy, can they sing! In seven annual performances, the Choir of Men and Boys displays tremendous talent from the entire Grand Rapids area. Approximately 25 boys make up the "performing choir" and 25 boys make up the "preparatory choir." They practice two or three times a week.

Your talented son might find this an exciting opportunity to develop into a real vocalist! Everyone will enjoy the choir's performances.

Dates/Hours: Watch for performance announcements.
Practices held after school
Admission: Varies
Phone: 245-4038
Address: Practices held at Sacred Heart School, performances at local auditoriums

Grand Rapids

Symphony Lollipops and Family Concerts

The Lollipops Concerts introduce preschoolers to the symphony by combining music with storytelling in 30-minute performances. The concerts are performed one day in the spring and one day in the fall at various area high schools.

The Family Concerts present music for all ages in three educational concerts, with free hands-on activities for children before each one. Concerts are approximately one hour long.

Dates/Hours:	Lollipops: 10 A.M.–11:30 A.M. Family Concerts: January, March, November, Sundays at 3 P.M. Call for specific dates
Admission:	Lollipops $3 per person; Family Concerts $6–$12
Phone:	454-9451
Address:	DeVos Hall, downtown Grand Rapids

Grand Rapids

Kindermusik

This music education program for the very young provides opportunities to move, explore, and be expressive. It also promotes social interaction and creativity.

Kindermusik Beginnings takes children 18 mos.–3 years old, and Kindermusik for the Young Child includes 4–7 year olds.

Dates/Hours: Monday and Tuesday
Admission: $90–$120 per semester
Phone: 361-5551
Address: Marywood Academy, 2025 E. Fulton Street, Grand Rapids. Locations in other cities too — check your local phone book

Grand Rapids

St. Cecilia Music Society

St. Cecilia's provides a wealth of opportunity for nurturing the talent of area youth in vocal and instrumental music. The society is a major center for all who enjoy listening to and performing music.

St. Cecilia's offers a wide variety of classes and lessons, including Music Discovery for 4–8 year olds. Older children might enjoy Music Adventures. Courses meet weekly for nine months and include music of all styles with rhythm, movement, singing, playing, and listening.

Dates/Hours: Music Discovery and Music Adventures meet on Tuesdays, October–December or February–April

Admission: $65–$80 per semester for classes; call for information about private lessons or choir

Phone: 459-2224

Address: 24 Ransom NE, downtown Grand Rapids

Grand Rapids

Youth Symphony

The Youth Symphony cultivates talented young instrumentalists. Many of southwestern Michigan's most accomplished and professionally successful artists enjoyed early ensemble experience with the Youth Symphony.

Auditions are required for membership. The symphony holds clinics and two annual performances in addition to weekly practices.

Dates/Hours:	Practices September–May: Mondays 7:15–9:15 P.M.
Admission:	$350
Phone:	459-2224
Address:	24 Ransom Avenue at corner of Fulton, downtown Grand Rapids

Holland

Youth Orchestra and Youth Chorale

Sponsored by the Holland Area Arts Council, the Youth Chorale pulls together the top 70 3rd–8th-grade students for Chorale practice and two performances each year. A one-year commitment is required.

Under the HAAC umbrella, the Youth Orchestra is made up of the top 70 5th–12th-grade brass, wind, and string instrumentalists in the Holland area. They play challenging musical pieces, participate in sectional workshops with area adult musicians, and perform in two formal concerts each year.

HAAC also organizes many free family-oriented performances and concerts each summer in various locations.

Phone: Holland Area Arts Council: 396-3276

Kalamazoo

Junior Symphony

The Junior Symphony nurtures junior musicians at all levels!

Early-elementary string students may, upon a teacher's recommendation, join the Training Orchestra. Approximately 30 children belong to this group.

Seventy-six string musicians play in the Prep String Orchestra, with performances in December and April. Junior high and high schoolers belong.

The final step, Junior Symphony Orchestra, is made up of 85 strings, winds, and percussionists who practice every Saturday morning and hold three concerts per year. Membership is made up of high school students, by audition only.

Dates/Hours:	Call for information
Admission:	Adults $3; students and seniors $1; under 5 free
Phone:	349-7557
Address:	714 S. Westnedge, Kalamazoo

Kalamazoo

Symphony Orchestra

Although the Kalamazoo Symphony plays mostly for adult audiences, it does sponsor a Family Discovery Series, with two performances each year just for families. Call for themes and dates.

In addition, the symphony's outreach program exposes thousands of schoolchildren to symphonic music. Its professional musicians give 200 performances each year.

Dates/Hours: Call for information
Admission: $1–$15
Phone: 387-2300 for tickets
Address: 426 S. Park Street, Kalamazoo

33

Muskegon

Blue Lake Fine Arts Camp

From mid-June to late August, you can listen to internationally known artists performing in a wooded natural setting on the shores of Little Blue Lake. Families are invited!

Blue Lake has highly acclaimed 12-day sessions for 5th–12th-grade children. Call for a brochure.

Dates/Hours:	June–August, call for performance schedule
Admission:	$3 general admission
Phone:	894-1966
Address:	U.S. 31, Russell Road exit, Muskegon, follow signs

EDUCATIONAL
ACTIVITIES

EDUCATIONAL ACTIVITIES

Books

Great Bookstores for Kids

Children of all ages enjoy reading and listening to books about their special interests. Books are excellent gifts for younger children; try bookstore gift certificates for upper-elementary kids and high schoolers.

We have found a great selection of bookstores, and the folks in these stores will gladly recommend books for your children. Check with your area bookstore for story hours (usually geared to specific age groups), author visits, summer reading programs, and children's play/reading areas.

Battle Creek:

B. Dalton Bookseller
Lakeview Square Mall
979-3700
Children's books take up the back half of store.

Bethel Bookstore
5700 Beckley Road
979-8020
Sunday school games

Lantern Book & Bible
25½ Urbandale Plaza
963-1962
Children's books, games, tapes, trinkets.

Benton Harbor–St. Joseph:

ABC Christian Book Center
8980 S. US 31-33, Berrien Springs
471-7331

Andrews University
Grove Street, Berrien Springs
471-3287

B. Dalton Bookseller
Orchards Mall, Benton Harbor
926-8259

Once Upon a Time
515 Pleasant, St. Joseph
983-5055

Grand Rapids:

Baker Book House
2768 E. Paris SE
957-3110

Breton Village Mall
942-9880

Grand Village Mall
249-8940

38

Book Tree
6431 28th SE
949-4220
Large children's section, many books for families

Family Bookstores
4196 Plainfield
363-4893

Woodland Mall
949-8892

2575 28th Street SW, Wyoming
531-0540
Religious books, music, toys, games, children's gift items

Images Books
813 Franklin SE
241-5909
African-American books, good children's selection

Little Professor Books
2165 Wealthy SE, East Grand Rapids
776-1616
Children's play/reading area

Pooh's Corner
Breton Village Mall
942-9887
Children's play/reading area, author visits, story times

Schuler Books
2975 28th Street SE
942-2561
Children's reading area, summer reading program

Waldenbooks
North Kent Mall
363-7734

Woodland Mall
957-9080
Children's and young adult book section

Webster's Books
3848 28th Street SE
285-7055
Large children's section

Grand Haven:

The Bookman
715 Washington
846-3520
Children's section

Holland:

Baker Book House
Cedar Village Mall
396-7001

West Shore Mall
393-2040

Pooh's Corner
48 East 8th
396-7411
Specializes in children's books; variety of activities and special events

Books

Athena Book Shop
300 S. Kalamazoo Mall, downtown
342-4508 or

Owl's Nest for Children
1-800-427-9257
Large children's book section

B. Dalton Bookseller
Crossroads Mall
327-0111
Children's reading corner

Eighth Day Bookstore
901 S. Westnedge
345-9665
Children's reading corner

John W. Rollins Books
6414 South Westnedge, Portage
323-3800
Large children's section

Lantern Book & Bible
4421 S. Westnedge
381-2230
Children's books and games

Waldenbooks
5052 W. Main, Oshtemo
342-4911
Special activities

EDUCATIONAL ACTIVITIES

Books

41

Book Nook
Park Row Mall
733-2850
Children's games, puzzles, and books

First Edition
7 Center, Muskegon Heights
733-2176
Children's books and comic books

Hage's Christian Supplies
888 Terrace
722-2146
*Religious and nonreligious books, games and
activities, homework helps*

Pages Hallmark
3255-A Colby, Whitehall
893-0707

EDUCATIONAL ACTIVITIES

Books

42

In addition to providing learning materials and books for enjoyment, libraries feature story hours for toddlers and preschoolers, educational computer games, visits by children's authors, bookmobiles, and summer reading programs.

Many libraries also present special programs and entertainment during the school year. The Kalamazoo Public Library, for example, runs "Spring Break Express," and the Kent County Public Library offers "Special Storytimes" during Christmas vacation.

Kids can have fun becoming familiar with the library's resources through **SLICK** (Super Library Information Club for Kids), an award-winning program operated by the Kent County Library System that takes kids on a 30-minute scavenger hunt through the library. Membership cards are awarded after the hunt.

To help kids choose books according to their reading level and special interests, **Bookbrain,** a user-friendly computer workstation session, gives them personalized computer printouts of books they might enjoy.

Call the Kent County Library System at 336-3250 for a schedule and registration information for these two programs.

Dates/Hours: Check with your local library
Admission: Free

43

EDUCATIONAL ACTIVITIES

Books

EDUCATIONAL ACTIVITIES

Museums

Battle Creek

Kimball House Museum

The Kimball House Museum is a Queen Anne-style home built in 1886 and deeded to the city of Battle Creek in 1966. The Historical Society has authentically furnished the first floor, four upstairs rooms, and a Pioneer Room using community contributions and volunteer efforts. Kimball House also features temporary exhibits.

The children's room contains hand-carved toys from the late 18th and early 19th centuries. Vintage clothing — beaded gowns, long baby dresses (worn by both boys and girls), hats, and Prince Alberts coats — all draw the kids' attention.

Good times to plan visits with children might be during June's Strawberry Festival, October's Harvest Festival, or the Christmas Open House.

Dates/Hours:	Tuesday–Saturday 12:30–4:30. Tours by special arrangement
Admission:	Free. Historical Society memberships available
Phone:	966-2496
Address:	196 Capital Avenue NE, Battle Creek

Battle Creek

Kingman Museum of Natural History

Three floors are loaded with hands-on exhibits. Grind corn in a Native American exhibit, walk through the layers of rocks and minerals in the crust of the earth, look at fossils, and find prehistoric life. Animal ecology and the "Wonders of Life" also merit attention, and don't miss the dinosaur in the lower level's Natural Science exhibit.

Visit the museum's planetarium to explore astronomy and space science. Geared for ages 4 and over, the planetarium shows run 25 minutes in length, Saturdays (1–3 P.M.) and Sundays (1:30–3 P.M.).

The museum also holds special group programs, geared to age level and topic of interest, and a "Pioneer Life" summer camp. It is conveniently located in the Leila Arboretum (see "The Great Outdoors").

Dates/Hours:	Tuesday–Saturday 9–5, Sunday 1–5
	Open Monday in July and August
Admission:	Adults $2; students 3–18 years $1
	2 and under free. Planetarium $1 extra
Phone:	965-5117
Address:	W. Michigan at 20th Street (east of M-37), northwest of downtown Battle Creek

Grand Haven

Tri-Cities Historical Museum

Housed in downtown Grand Haven's historic railroad de-
pot, the Tri-Cities Museum emphasizes themes of local
importance in its permanent exhibits: lumbering, pioneer
life, Victorian life, local industry, and resorts. The Coast
Guard history rates its own gallery.

Popular temporary exhibits have included those
about the Civil War and World War II. The general store
and corner grocery deserve a peek, too.

Dates/Hours:	Memorial Day – Labor Day:
	Tuesday–Saturday 10–9:30
	Winter: Tuesday–Friday 10–5,
	Saturday–Sunday 12–4
Admission:	Adults $1; children under 17 free
Phone:	842-0700
Address:	Ferry's Landing Mouth, 7 N. Harbor,
	Grand Haven

EDUCATIONAL ACTIVITIES

Museums

47

Grand Rapids

Gerald R. Ford Museum

Gerald R. Ford, 38th president of the United States, is paid a handsome tribute through this museum and its history-oriented programs. Ford's life and dedication to public service are highlighted.

Younger children might enjoy learning about President Ford's years as a Boy Scout and athlete, and a reproduction of his Oval Office and gifts from other heads of state rate "must-sees" for all ages. Kids, don't lean on the glass enclosures; security guards disapprove. There's also a Bicentennial section and gift shop.

Three videos and one 30-minute film are available for viewing, and the museum provides guided tours for 5th-grade school groups.

Dates/Hours: Monday–Saturday 9–4:45, Sunday 12–4:45
Admission: Adults $3;
children under 16 free;
seniors $1.50
Phone: 451-9263
Address: 303 Pearl Street, just off US 131 Pearl Street exit, downtown Grand Rapids

48

Grand Rapids

Children's Museum Exhibits

Traveling hands-on science exhibits are featured in various area locations in Grand Rapids, such as the public library and area malls.

A permanent home for the Children's Museum is expected to open in downtown Grand Rapids in December 1995. To be a part of this effort, call 940-1475.

Dates/Hours: Permanent facility hours to be
                 determined
Admission: Free
Phone: 940-1745 ext. 5576
Address: Future location off Fulton Street,
                downtown Grand Rapids

Grand Rapids

Grand Rogue Living History Encampment

Visit authentic wartime military campsites to find out how soldiers and their families lived and survived. Watch volunteers in accurate costumes shoot cannons, fight battles, and demonstrate military and camp life in reenactments of various periods, including the French and Indian War, the Revolutionary War, and the Civil War. Kids who are bored with textbook history will be tantalized.

The Living History Encampment is sponsored by the West Michigan Living History and Educational Association.

The Grand Rogue Campground offers many other activities, including canoeing and tubing (see "The Great Outdoors").

Dates/Hours:	Memorial Day, Fourth of July, Labor Day, and one mid-September weekend
Admission:	Donations gratefully accepted
Phone:	361-1053
Address:	Grand Rogue Campground: U.S. 131 to exit 91 (Comstock Park), 4 miles east on West River Drive

Grand Rapids

Roger B. Chaffee Planetarium

Located in the Van Andel Museum Center, Chaffee Planetarium is housed in one of two eye-catching pavilions. Using state-of-the-art audio-visual and electronic technology, the planetarium features sky shows on a wide range of topics — about stars, planets, comets, constellations, and black holes.

Watch for public announcements, and choose age-appropriate shows for your children (otherwise they'll get antsy). Set aside plenty of time to visit the the rest of the new Van Andel Museum, too.

The planetarium visit is also a good school trip; make advance reservations.

Dates/Hours: Usually Friday and Saturday evenings, and Saturday and Sunday afternoons; field trips by special arrangement
Admission: Adults $3.50; children/seniors $1.75 (includes museum admission)
Phone: 456-3200, 456-3985
Address: 272 Pearl Street NW, just off U.S. 131 Pearl Street exit, downtown Grand Rapids

Grand Rapids

Van Andel Museum Center

With four areas of greatest emphasis — the Spillman carousel and the planetarium (both housed in tremendous circular pavilions), Furniture City, and a reincarnated 1890s Gaslight Village — Grand Rapids' new public museum is an educational and architectural wonder.

Visitors gain a gorgeous view of the city and the Grand River from the museum. But here's the REAL kid pleaser: a huge blue whale skeleton hanging in splendor! "Habitats and the Natural Environment" and "Anishinabek" (Native Americans) are two important permanent exhibits.

Classrooms, used for after-school educational programs and other seminars, overlook the river.

Dates/Hours: Monday–Friday 10–5,
              Saturday–Sunday 1–5
Admission: Adults $2.50; children 4–15 years $.75;
              under 4 free
Phone: 456-3977
Address: 272 Pearl Street NW, just off the Pearl
              Street exit at U.S 131

EDUCATIONAL ACTIVITIES

Museums

Hastings

Charlton Park Village & Museum

Take a guided or self-guided tour of Charlton Park's 17-building village for a glimpse of western Michigan towns as they stood 100 years ago, and then plan to enjoy the 332-acre recreation area.

Charlton Park's Recreation Area, situated on the Thornapple River and Lake Charlton, is a wonderful place to swim, boat, water-ski, fish, hike, picnic, and play softball and volleyball or playground games.

Charlton Park also puts on Civil War reenactments during the first weekend in June as well as an Old Fashioned Fourth of July, Folk Life Festival, All Hallow's Evening, Of Christmas Past, and various auto shows. Educational field trips are also available.

Dates/Hours: Mid-May to mid-October: all open.
Winter: museum, educational programs, recreation area open

Admission: Barry County residents free. Nonresident adults $3; children 5–15 $1; under 5 free. Extra charge for special events

Phone: 945-3775, call for complete schedule

Address: M-37 south of Hastings to M-79. Turn east, 4 miles, north on Charlton Park Road

EDUCATIONAL ACTIVITIES

Museums

53

Hickory Corners

Gilmore Classic Car Club Museum

The kids will love hearing your stories about "the way cars were" when you grew up as you tour the Gilmore Classic Car Museum. Show them the the most complete collection of antique and classic vehicles in North America.

Five historic red barns house over 100 automobiles, including Rolls Royces, Packards, a 1984 Indy Pace Car, and an 1899 Locomobile. Also, look for The Green Hornet and Disney's Gnome Mobile.

Bring a picnic and enjoy the 90-acre rural setting. The museum also hosts numerous car shows and swap meets, and is available for group gatherings.

Dates/Hours:	Mid-May through mid-October, 9–5 daily
Admission:	Adults $6; seniors $5. Children 12 and under accompanied by parent are free
Phone:	671-5089
Address:	6865 Hickory Road (on M-43), Hickory Corners, 16 miles northeast of Kalamazoo

EDUCATIONAL ACTIVITIES

Museums

Holland

The Holland Museum

This extensive collection of artifacts from both the Old and New Worlds includes Dutch decorative arts, a doll house, and a hand-carved carousel. Exhibits center around such periods as Holland's beginnings in 1847 as a "kolonie," the great fire of 1871, and its current status as a flourishing, diverse community.

Community pride is evident here, and adults and older students will appreciate Holland's fascinating history and thousands of artifacts.

Dates/Hours: Daily 10–5, Thursday 10–8, Sunday 2–5
Closed Tuesday
Admission: Adults $3; students and seniors $2;
preschoolers free
Phone: 392-9084
Address: I-196 to exit 52, 5 miles west to 31 West
10th Street, Holland

Holland

Poll Museum of Transportation

You'll find an outstanding collection of antique and classic cars, fire trucks, bicycles, coaches, tractor engines, and model trains at the Poll Museum.

Be sure to look for the 1906 Mercedes, 1917 Coco-mobile, and 1921 Pierce Arrow roadster!

Dates/Hours:	May 1–October 1: daily 9–5
Admission:	Adults $2; children 10–12 years $.50; under 10 free
Phone:	392-2389
Address:	U.S. 31 to New Holland Street, four miles north

Kalamazoo

Aviation History Museum

The "Kalamazoo Air Zoo" houses a group of beautifully restored World War II fighters: the Curtiss P-40 Warhawk and the four Grumman Cats (Wildcat, Hellcat, Tigercat, and Bearcat), as well as other military aircraft. The 41,000 square-foot museum also houses memorabilia and scale models that present a complete picture of WWII and Allied airpower.

From May to September, tour the Air Zoo's famed Restoration Center to watch vintage aircrafts being restored. The center's aircraft have won major awards at national air show competitions.

Many of the planes are airworthy and participate in air shows throughout the U.S. and Canada. A "Flight of the Day" program permits one flight each summer day.

Dates/Hours: Monday–Saturday 10–6, Wednesday
10–8, Sunday 1–6. October–April:
Monday–Saturday 10–5, Sunday 1–5
Admission: Adults $5; children 6–15 $3
5 and under free
Phone: 382-6555
Address: 2101 E. Milham Road, Kalamazoo

Kalamazoo

Challenger Learning Center

The Challenger Learning Center, a part of the Kalamazoo Public Museum that opened in 1993, allows students to become part of a space "mission" through the use of a space station simulator.

During 45-minute **Mini Mission** simulations, your child and other crew members are assigned stations and work to accomplish their mission. Kids must be at least 12 years old or in 6th grade to be unaccompanied by an adult. No pre-registration is required, but numbers are strictly limited.

The space station simulator and mission control are keys to a monthly three-hour **Full Mission** program which includes training, team selection, and mission. Kids collect data, conduct experiments, and launch a probe. Minimum age is 12 years or 6th grade. Make reservations early.

Dates/Hours:	Both run one Saturday afternoon per month
Admission:	Mini-mission: 8–11 years $1.50; 12 years and older $3
	Full mission: $20
Phone:	345-7092
Address:	315 S. Rose Street, second floor of Kalamazoo Public Library until the new museum opens in 1995

Kalamazoo

Hans Baldauf Planetarium

The Kalamazoo Public Museum's Planetarium offers regular programs free of charge on Wednesdays, Fridays, and weekends. The programs place emphasis on audience participation and on information you can use when stargazing in your backyard.

Nominal fees are charged for special programs, which rotate monthly. Large groups should call ahead for reservations.

Dates/Hours: Wednesday and Friday 4 P.M.,
                    Saturday–Sunday 2:30 and 3:30 P.M.
Admission: Most programs are free; monthly features
                    $1.50 for adults, $1 for children
Phone: 345-7092
Address: 315 South Rose, second floor of public
                    library. In 1995 it will move to north end
                    of downtown mall

EDUCATIONAL ACTIVITIES

Museums

59

Kalamazoo Public Museum

There are many great reasons to visit the Kalamazoo Public Museum, but none so compelling for kids as its 2,300-year-old mummy — formerly a wealthy Egyptian woman!

The Kalamazoo Public Museum offers hands-on explorations into science and technology (InventiCenter), and local history and culture (Kazoo! Kazoo!). Its Special Exhibitions Gallery features traveling shows and temporary exhibitions.

Children are the museum's main focus: check out the hands-on Kids' Corner and preschool and general-interest programs. The Worldworks program allows visitors to borrow any one of 1,320 cases filled with items pertaining to world cultures, science, and technology. Read about the museum's planetarium and Challenger Learning Center elsewhere in this section.

Dates/Hours:	September–May: Tuesday–Saturday 9–5, Wednesday 9–9, Sunday 1–5 Summer: Tuesday–Saturday 9–5
Admission:	Free. Small admission sometimes charged for special exhibitions and some planetarium programs
Phone:	345-7092
Address:	315 S. Rose Street, at South Street. On second floor of Public Library in downtown Kalamazoo

Kalamazoo

The New Museum

Scheduled to open in 1995, the New Museum will cover more than twice Kalamazoo Public Museum's 30,000 square feet.

The New Museum is envisioned as a learning-resource center for science, history, technology, social studies, cultural awareness, and health. It will utilize many of the public museum's current artifacts, but it is also adding new high-tech features, such as interpretive exhibits activated by touchscreens with video modules, holograms, and hands-on displays.

The Digistar Theater and Planetarium, Interactive Lecture Hall, Teacher Resource Center, Inventor's Workshop, Theater of Industry and Science, and preschoolers' Discovery Center will also be part of the museum.

Dates/Hours: September–May: Tuesday–Saturday 9–5, Wednesday 9–9, Sunday 1–5 Summer: Tuesday–Saturday 9–5
Admission: Free; donations welcome
Phone: 345-7092, or call information for new number
Address: Arcadia Commons, north end of Kalamazoo Mall

Muskegon

Carr-Fles Planetarium — Muskegon

The planetarium is open to the public every Tuesday and Thursday at 7 P.M. free of charge. Four shows, including "To Worlds Beyond" and "Cosmic Whisper," rotate throughout the year, with seating for 46 available. Teachers may choose from a dozen interesting school programs and schedule visits with their classes. Call three weeks ahead to make reservations.

Groups of 15 may schedule private programs during the day; evening groups of twenty can be accommodated. No shows are given from Friday through Sunday.

These are great programs for kids over 8 years old. Younger children may attend if they can sit still for 45 minutes. It's dark in the planetarium, and they won't be able to leave after the show starts.

Dates/Hours: Tuesdays and Thursdays 7 P.M.,
             or by arrangement
Admission: Free
Phone: 777-0289
Address: Muskegon Community College:
             221 S. Quarterline Road, Muskegon

Muskegon

Muskegon County Museum

Muskegon is a city with a past, a future, and a very fine museum! With five permanent galleries, the museum is able to showcase the city's Indian fur-trading and lumbering history, offer a great natural history exhibit (including a dinosaur skeleton), and honor the area's finest athletes in the Muskegon Sports Hall of Fame.

Our kids' favorite gallery, though, was the interactive, hands-on "Body Works." A human skeleton, child's chest X-ray, and test of the five senses were just the beginning! Even the little kids thoroughly enjoyed our two-hour museum visit.

The museum offers school programs, lending kits, "Sci-Fi" for 6–12-year-old girls, a summer day camp called "EnviroWorks," and an array of other educational programs.

Dates/Hours: Monday–Friday 9:30–4:30,
Saturday–Sunday 12:30–4:30. Tours by
appointment
Admission: Free; donations welcome
Phone: 722-0278
Address: 430 West Clay at Fourth, 1 block west of
Hackley Park, downtown Muskegon

Muskegon

Heritage Tour

Muskegon was once a booming lumber town. Visitors may walk through area museums and lumber barons' mansions as volunteers in period costumes provide commentary and insight into Muskegon's colorful past during the $2\frac{1}{2}$-hour Heritage Tour. It all ends with a Victorian tea and refreshments.

While the Heritage Tour is very interesting, we recommend it only for older children because of its length.

Groups are welcome any time. Bus tours are also available for up to 44 people.

Dates/Hours: June–August on Wednesdays and
              Sundays 1:30 P.M.
Admission: Adults $7; children 5–18 years $2. Adults
              with group $5; reservations needed
Phone: 737-5767
Address: Begins at Muskegon County Museum,
              430 West Clay

Muskegon

Science Resource Center

With the aim of increasing the availability of science in the Muskegon area, the Muskegon County Museum now has its own Science Resource Center. Families may conduct hands-on science experiments and learn more about social and environmental topics. The preschool section features a dinosaur fantasy land.

The Science Resource Center will also become a regional training center for the county's teachers, and many topical programs — such as Weather and Electricity — are available to groups. EnviroWorks summer day camps also fall into the Resource Center's domain. (It's free. First-come, first-served.)

Dates/Hours: Monday–Friday 9:30–4:30.
              Weekends 12:30–4:30
Admission: Free
Phone: 722-0278
Address: Muskegon County Museum: 4th and
              Clay, Muskegon

Muskegon

USS *Silversides* and Maritime Museum

America's most famous submarine, USS *Silversides,* now resides in Muskegon, and is open from April to October for tours and overnight stays.

Silversides completed 14 war patrols and sank 23 ships (third highest of all subs in U.S. history) with the mission of stopping raw materials and supplies from entering Japan. Other missions included mine laying and reconnaissance and the rescue of two downed aviators. *Silversides* was considered extremely lucky — only one man was lost in all battle actions.

Public and group tours are available, as are youth group overnight trips. In the past seven years more than 20,000 kids have bunked down in *Silversides'* cramped quarters and explored the sub fore to aft.

Dates/Hours:	April–October Saturday–Sunday 10–5:30
	May and September weekdays 1–5:30
	June–August daily 10–5:30
Admission:	Adults $3.50; children under 12 $1.50; seniors $2
Phone:	755-1230
Address:	740 W. Western Avenue on Muskegon Lake, Muskegon

(margin) EDUCATIONAL ACTIVITIES

(margin) *Museums*

South Haven

Michigan Maritime Museum

This harborfront museum offers a series of exhibits on Great Lakes maritime history, from Native American dugout canoes to today's watercraft. Coast Guard and recreational boating histories are two themes of the rotating exhibits.

A maritime research library is open by appointment. The gift shop is well stocked with resource materials, model-boat kits, and jewelry.

Tours for groups of all ages are available (call in advance), as well as public lectures and waterfront events.

Dates/Hours:	Wednesday–Saturday 10–4
Admission:	Adults $2.50; children 5–12 years $1.50
Phone:	637-8078
Address:	I-196 to exit 20, 1½ miles west on Dyckman Avenue just west of the Drawbridge, South Haven

St. Joseph

Curious Kids Museum

This family-oriented museum has a sand table (hurray, toddlers!) with measuring and sifting devices, an extensive selection of career costumes for your future workers, and a simulated orchard where kids can pick and load apples into a hopper and crank the conveyor.

Be sure to check out the replica of a double-decked ship and cargo to be loaded (by your curious kids, or course), a climbable two-story dinosaur, and the giant bubbles.

Dates/Hours: Wednesday–Saturday 10–5,
              Sunday 12–5
Admission: Adults $3; children $2; under 2 free
Phone: 983-2543
Address: 415 Lake Street, St. Joseph

Whitehall

White River Lighthouse Museum

Climb the spiral staircase to the top of the lighthouse to see a stunning view of Lake Michigan and surrounding sand dunes. Then have a look at Great Lakes ship relics and navigational charts. Be sure to examine one of the multifaceted lenses used to create coded signals. Approaching mariners used them to identify the harbor and to maneuver safely to port.

Dates/Hours: May 30–August 30: Tuesday–Friday
                      11–5, weekends 12–6
Admission: Adults $1; 10–18 years $.50;
                      9 and under free
Phone: 894-8265
Address: 6199 Murray Road, Whitehall. Off U.S.
                      31, 5 miles toward White Lake

Community Programs

Grand Rapids

Behind the Scenes

This monthly children's program offers 4–12-year-old children hands-on experiences with some of Grand Rapids' best companies. Past visits have included banks, restaurants, movie theaters, and veterinary clinics.

Sponsored by *Our Children* magazine, the "Place of the Month" visits are usually scheduled for Saturday mornings. They are informative and age appropriate.

The magazine is distributed free to grocery stores and kids' stores in Kent, Ottawa, Allegan, Muskegon, and Newaygo counties.

Dates/Hours:	Look for schedules and registration forms in *Our Children* magazine
Admission:	$5 per child
Phone:	940-8051
Address:	Locations vary each month. Write *Our Children*, Box 1101, Grand Rapids, 49501 for information

EDUCATIONAL ACTIVITIES

Community Programs

71

Grand Rapids

Community Enrichment Day

As part of Grand Rapids' Celebration on the Grand, local cultural and educational institutions offer free admission on Community Enrichment Day. Check out your old favorites, or take the family for a new adventure.

Free bus shuttles run from GUS lots to the John Ball Zoo, Gerald R. Ford Museum, the Art Museum, Van Andel Museum, historical Voigt House, Chaffee Planetarium, public library, or Belknap Ice Arena from 10 A.M. to 5 P.M.

Begin the day, though, at the Community Breakfast, 9–11 A.M., at Grand Rapids Community College Cafeteria. Admission is $2.

Dates/Hours:	Second Sunday in September, last day of Celebration on the Grand
Admission:	Free
Phone:	456-2675
Address:	Most locations are downtown Grand Rapids; call ahead for directions

Grand Rapids

"Sundays Are Special" Series

Explore national and world cultures through dance, music, folklore, masks, and sign language. A different topic is presented each Sunday by highly spirited actors.

Sponsored by the Council of Performing Arts for Children at the Van Andel Museum Center, the series is geared especially for families with preschool and elementary-age children.

Dates/Hours: Sundays in January and February: 1:30 and 2:30 P.M.
Admission: Adults $4.50; children $2.75, museum admission included
Phone: CPAC: 774-9922
Address: 272 Pearl Street NW. Pearl Street exit off U.S. 131

EDUCATIONAL ACTIVITIES

Community Programs

73

Greater Grand Rapids

West Michigan Science Festival

FINALLY, businesses and educators have organized a celebration of the contributions of science, math, and technology in our world today. This is a truly outstanding cooperative effort.

Students at all levels may select one- to four-hour activities involving an enormous variety of topics, from "Learning to Fly and Becoming a Pilot" to "Veterinary Medicine and Surgery" to "Introduction to Community Planning." Organizers plan over 100 interesting events and stress the value of interacting with real people in real jobs that involve math and science skills.

Parents may register children individually for these activities, scheduled during daytime and evening hours. Teachers may also arrange field trips to Science Festival activities.

Dates/Hours:	Third week in April. Booklet/registration form available at schools and libraries
Admission:	Free, or nominal fee
Phone:	895-2515 for questions. Must register by mail
Address:	Various businesses and schools throughout the Greater Grand Rapids area

Kalamazoo

Kids Wanna Have Fun and Be Safe Day

Various community organizations share health, safety, and educational resources and information with parents and children in this carnival-like atmosphere.

Forty exhibits, hands-on activities, clowns, and door prizes help parents and children pick up safety tips in a fun way. For example, fire safety (stop, drop, and roll) is a biggie.

Organized by the Breakfast Optimist Club of Kalamazoo to promote the many safe activities offered in the Kalamazoo area, the event draws nearly 2,000 participants annually!

Dates/Hours: Last Saturday in March
Admission: Free
Phone: 344-7371
Address: Indoors at Kalamazoo County
             Fairgrounds; call to verify location

EDUCATIONAL ACTIVITIES

Supplies

Grand Rapids

Creative Learning Center

The vast variety of educational toys, puzzles, books, games, and kits here will heighten your child's interest in math, science, arts, and crafts.

CLC also has an Odds & Ends program. For a small donation, you may fill a brown paper bag with scrap art materials provided by area companies. This is especially good for Scout and class projects and for at-home pre-school artists.

Dates/Hours: Monday-Saturday 9–9
Admission: Free to browse
Phone: 243-3551
Address: Breton Center, southwest corner of
             Breton Road and 28th Street SE, Grand
             Rapids

Grand Rapids

Grow & Learn

This great educational store offers fresh ideas, games, and activities to liven up the classroom or home. Stop in and browse — you could be there all day!

<table>
<tr><td>Dates/Hours:</td><td>Monday–Saturday 10–9, closed Sunday</td></tr>
<tr><td>Admission:</td><td>Free, but you may find some treasures to buy</td></tr>
<tr><td>Phone:</td><td>942-7621</td></tr>
<tr><td>Address:</td><td>Eastbrook Mall: 3655 28th Street SE, Grand Rapids</td></tr>
</table>

Supplies

Grand Rapids

The Teacher's Store

Your area may have the equivalent of the Teacher's Store; if so, check it out! You will find great gifts for teachers — they might appreciate classroom additions instead of perfume, bubble bath, and coffee mugs.

Even more interesting are typical teaching materials that can be put to work in your home. We have used teachers' educational posters in our kids' bathroom for years, and like it or not, they know where the U.S. states and Canadian provinces are located. The human anatomy is currently posted at eye level, and plant and animal classifications adorn the sink. It's a good idea to have them laminated at your local print shop, too — then they'll last forever.

A bit of imagination goes a long way!

Dates/Hours:	Monday–Saturday 9:30–6
Admission:	Free browsing
Phone:	949-7942
Address:	2845 Lake Eastbrook Boulevard SE.
	South off 28th Street, Grand Rapids

CAMPS AND CLASSES

CAMPS AND CLASSES

Babysitter Training Clinics

Typically geared for ages 10 to 14, training classes teach basic infant and child care, ideas for entertaining and playing with children, and how to make decisions in an emergency. Classes are often held in two two-hour sessions.

Some programs award certificates upon completion, and some offer an option to be placed on a community list of available babysitters. Not only will your kids become better babysitters, but they can also provide this handy credential when looking for sitting jobs.

Classes are offered through the American Red Cross, recreation and community education departments, and hospitals.

Dates/Hours: Variable
Admission: Approximately $10–$30
Phone: Check your phone book for local numbers

4-H Programs in Western Michigan

4-H is alive and well, both in rural western Michigan and in urban areas. The 4-H creed establishes high values and self-esteem in 6–19 year olds.

The 4-H organization sponsors a variety of programs and classes, including music, drum and bugle, sewing, computers, rabbits, and horse clubs.

Urban 4-H is currently building resources to further expand its offerings, and already runs programs in Calhoun, Kalamazoo, Kent, Muskegon, Ottawa, and Van Buren counties. A very worthwhile program, 4-H can always use adult volunteers and donations. Call for information.

Dates/Hours: Great variation; call for schedules
Admission: Usually free
Phone: 336-3265 in Grand Rapids; check local phone listings
Address: 1329 Franklin SE, Grand Rapids

CAMPS AND CLASSES

84

Lifeguard Training and Water Safety Training

Kids who are at least 15 years old may become Red Cross-certified lifeguards, and those 17 and older qualify for Water Safety Instructor certification. Classes are held periodically through local YMCAs and recreation departments.

Students must pass a certification test at the end of the course. Recertification is available through refresher courses.

Swimming ability is a must! Lifeguarding and teaching swimming lessons make good summer or part-time jobs for students, and the CPR training included in the lifeguarding course provides valuable knowledge for many kinds of emergency situations.

Dates/Hours: Call for schedules
Admission: Varies
Phone: American Red Cross

Kidz' Express Science Workshops

Science IS fun and exciting, and two Wizards at Work are willing to prove it. Invite them to your school, or Scout or youth group, and watch them do hands-on experiments that kids can repeat at home.

The Wizards tailor their workshops to groups' ages and needs. They have worked with preschoolers through 6th-graders, and have gained national exposure for their presentations.

Organizations within the Kalamazoo Public Library district may arrange through the library to have a workshop free of charge. Out-of-district groups should contact *Kidz' Express* (a publication for kids) to arrange a presentation. Fees vary depending on a group's needs. Also available are private writing workshops for children's organizations.

Dates/Hours: By arrangement
Admission: Free for groups in library district;
              otherwise, fees vary
Phone: Kalamazoo Library: 342-4859.
              Kids' Express: 373-5505
Address: Your location

CAMPS AND CLASSES

86

Preschool Programs

In addition to this sampling of programs for preschool-age children, contact your area recreation department, gymnastics facility, or YMCA for ideas. Many zoos, museums, and preschools also operate summer day camps. A few are Canterbury Creek Farms (Ada), Franciscan Farms (Lowell), and John Ball Zoo (Grand Rapids).

Grand Rapids:

Family Fun Gymnastics Centre
6375 S. Division
455-0475

Gym Rompers Superior Gymnastics
5106 Bridle Creek Court
455-3151

Gymboree
Eastbrook Community Center
372-6140 or 1-800-339-7716
Seven class levels by age, beginning at 0–3 months. Hands-on games, activities, and tyke-sized play equipment. Skilled, enthusiastic teachers. Approximately $45 per eight-week session.

Gymnastic Company
2310 29th Street SE
241-1296
Preschool movement classes 1–6 years, performance team, birthday parties, field trips.

Gymnastiks Unlimited
Grand Village Mall, Grandville
534-6555
Birthday parties, field trips

Wiggles & Giggles
East Grand Rapids Recreation Department
949-1750
Creative expression through tumbling, music, and props. Two age groups: $2\frac{1}{2}$-$3\frac{1}{2}$ and $3\frac{1}{2}$-$4\frac{1}{2}$. 45 minutes weekly for 11 weeks. Residents $25, nonresidents $35.

Kalamazoo:

Gymboree
1018 N. 7th
372-6140
See above.

Greater Kazoo World of Gymnastics
3754 Miller Road
381-5749
Tumblebears

Kids Gym
1424 West Centre, Portage
323-7657
Tumblekids, ages 1–5 years. Unique birthday parties and field trips.

Swimming, fishing, canoeing, horseback riding, camping, archery . . . funny counselors, funnier songs, and hilarious bugs — all are part of a kid's memories of summer camp.

Options include church-affiliated, Scout, and YMCA camps, but there are more! Four hundred camps are licensed by the state of Michigan, which has high standards for our kids' best interests. Eighty of these camps are further accredited by the American Camping Association. Some camps offer a mainstream experience, others are specialized.

Contact the Division of Child Welfare Licensing, Michigan Department of Social Services at (517) 373-8383. The ACA has a directory of Michigan's accredited camps; call 1-800-852-8368.

CAMPS AND CLASSES

Ada

Children's Repertory Workshop

Specifically for children ages 8 to 12 who are intensely interested in theater, the Children's Repertory Workshop provides top-notch theatrical education and entertainment "for children and by children."

Auditions are held in September, and approximately 25 children are selected to join the workshop. Students meet twice weekly from October to March, and stage two original productions and one tour show each year.

Participants will need rehearsal clothes and shoes.

Dates/Hours:	October–March: twice weekly. Performances given in December and March, plus school shows
Admission:	$300 per year; includes movement classes, costumes, and all other expenses
Phone:	452-7927
Address:	Northern Hills Middle School, 3775 Leonard NE, Ada

Grand Rapids

Children's Talent Center

Elementary-age children with special interests will sink their teeth into these eight-week classes in science, math, technology, foreign languages, and the arts.

Dates/Hours: After school; call for schedule
Admission: $85 per class
Phone: 949-6886
Address: Held at Third Reformed Church, 2060 Michigan NE

Grand Rapids

Children's Theatre Classes

Grand Rapids Civic Children's Theatre offers general acting classes and specialized workshops for children from age 8 to young adult. At the end of sessions, students put on impressive performances for parents, siblings, and friends.
These classes fill up fast, so register early!

Dates/Hours: After school and Saturdays during school year. One-week day camps (9 A.M.–3 P.M.) in summer.

Admission: Summer day camp tuition, $115; others vary

Phone: 456-9301

Address: 30 N. Division at Library, ½ block north of Fulton Street and Division, Grand Rapids

Grand Rapids

Computer Tots

Computers **will** play a large part in your child's future. These classes explore language, math, science, and art with kids ages 3 and up. The classes are kept small, and stimulate curiosity while preparing young children for the future.

A teacher will come equipped with hardware, software, and curriculum right to your day care, preschool or other community site across the United States.

Dates/Hours: By appointment
Admission: Call for information
Phone: (616) 791-7512
Address: P.O. Box 141454, Grand Rapids 49514

Grand Rapids

Fun-Tastiks Classes

Have fun through play with your special-needs child! Offered by the Comprehensive Therapy Center, Fun-Tastiks will build his or her physical, mental, and social confidence. Children are grouped in classes by age.

Dates/Hours: Call for schedule
Admission: $85 for eight weekly classes
Phone: 949-6886
Address: Held at Third Reformed Church, 2060
               Michigan SE, Grand Rapids

Grand Rapids

Kendall College Art Classes

Kendall College of Art and Design teams up with the Grand Rapids Art Museum to offer preschoolers through young adults a variety of art lessons.

Students visit the art museum for inspiration, then travel a few blocks to Kendall College to create — through painting, drawing, sculpting, or dance. Cartooning was an area of special interest for one of our kids, and Kendall has it!

Dates/Hours: Usually on Saturdays during school year; throughout the week during summer
Admission: $60 per class
Phone: 459-4676
Address: Kendall College, 11 N. Division, downtown Grand Rapids

Grand Rapids

Summer Therapy and Fun Camp

This special camp is intended for children receiving individualized treatment for speech and language, occupational, or physical therapy for oral, motor, thinking, or handwriting skills, or assistance in reading or auditory processing. Infants to teens are welcome. Campers participate in games, computer practice, arts and crafts, music and dance, singing, and drama.

Dates/Hours: Late June to early August,
Tuesday–Thursday 9 A.M.–12 NOON
Admission: Expensive, but grants may be available
Phone: 949-6886
Address: Third Reformed Church Building, 2060 Michigan SE (at Lakeside), Grand Rapids

CAMPS AND CLASSES

96

Kalamazoo

Art School at Kalamazoo Institute of Arts

Kalamazoo Institute of Arts offers a complete schedule of classes for kids and adults in all areas of art. Drawing, graphic design, printmaking, sculpture, photography, and other classes are presented by KIA's faculty artists.

Occasional short-term classes, preschool and senior sessions, and special groups are held by arrangement.

We still have a really ugly sculpture made many years ago in a KIA class. The teachers tried!

Dates/Hours: Varies; call for schedule
Admission: Varies by class and time of year
Fall/winter classes run 12 weeks; spring/summer, 6 weeks
Phone: 349-7775
Address: 314 South Park at Lovell, downtown Kalamazoo

Kalamazoo

Kalamazoo Area Math and Science Center

The Math and Science Center's summer classes aim to bring science, math, and computers down to earth — making them understandable and fun for kids. Fifty classes are offered for 1st–9th-graders on a wide variety of topics. Students attend one- or two-week sessions for two hours per day.

A junior high group might build model homes using its own blueprints and a given budget. Younger children may take "Kitchen Chemistry," while older students make "Chemical Creations."

During the school year, the Math and Science Center offers half-day advanced math, science, and computer classes for qualified students, granting full high school credit. Seventy-five students are accepted each year from a field of 350 applicants. It's an excellent program!

Dates/Hours:	Third week in June through the first week in August
Admission:	One-week session $40 Two-week session $60
Phone:	337-0004
Address:	600 W. Vine Street, Kalamazoo

Kentwood

Children's Creations

Located in the La Placita Shopping Center in Kentwood, Children's Creations is a unique program of after-school art and drama classes and a summer arts camp.

Geared for creative, energetic 3–16 year olds, classes are kept to a six-child maximum. Artist Janae Fowler keeps a file on each child and finds projects and media to suit him or her. Children who are in one of the hour-long classes may attend indefinitely, paying by the week.

Students are usually already interested in art, and some are very talented! Those who are unable to get to downtown's Kendall College for classes find Children's Creations a great alternative. Approximately 75 children attend the program.

Dates/Hours:	Monday, Tuesday, and Thursday after school. Drama workshops on Fridays
Admission:	3–6 years: $5/hour; 7–11 years: $6/hour; 12–16 years: $8/hour
Phone:	281-3443
Address:	La Placita Shopping Plaza, 1714 44th Street SE, one block east of Kalamazoo Avenue, Kentwood

Lowell

The Franciscan Child Development Center

Choose from a variety of programs for the whole family at the center's beautiful 212-acre farm near Lowell. The Franciscan Sisters offer a very well-run preschool program, seasonal one-day camps, and summer day camps.

Music classes for all ages are taught at the Franciscan Rhythms Music Studio, including private lessons on piano, harp, guitar, brass, woodwind, and percussion instruments. For school groups, the center offers many hands-on "Experience Programs," such as working the farms or orchards.

Two annual festivals take place: September's Fall Farm Festival, and April's Spring Arts Festival.

Dates/Hours: Call for programs, dates and directions
Admission: Varies
Phone: 897-7842
Address: 11650 Downes NE, Lowell

TOURS AND EXCURSIONS

Boat Cruises

Muskegon

The *Port City Princess,* a former Mackinac Island ferry, offers special event and theme cruises, like a kids' favorite — the PeeWee Pirate Cruise! Cruises run May–October by reservation; call 728-8387. Located at Western Avenue next to Hartshorn Marina.

Grand Haven

The *Harbor Steamer* is a sternwheel paddleboat that runs 1½-hour cruises on the Grand River and Spring Lake from mid-June to Labor Day. Call 842-8950 for reservations. 301 N. Harbor Drive, Chinook Pier.

Saugatuck

The *Star of Saugatuck,* an old-fashioned sternwheel paddleboat, runs 1½ hour narrated cruises on Lake Michigan from May to October. It leaves from Harbour Village, which has plenty of other attractions (see SS *Keewatin* in "Tours and Excursions"). Call 857-4261 for reservations.

Government in Action

These trips vary by location, so call your local institutions for information. Always schedule in advance.

Courthouse and Trial: Upper elementary and high school students can learn how our justice system works by seeing it in action. Excellent behavior and decorum are expected. Court dockets change frequently — even after arrangements have been made to view a trial — so call to verify the schedule.

Fire Station: Some fire stations have fire safety films in addition to tours. Children will see fire engines, and are sometimes allowed to sit in them. It makes a great pre-school/early-elementary school field trip! Our 2 year olds went, and a very nice firefighter turned on the lights and let them sit in the fire truck. The horn and siren would have scared the daylights out of them!

Hospital Tours

School classes, Scouts, and other organizations may arrange tours of your area hospitals.

Programs vary by hospital, from movies to hands-on activities to walk-throughs, so be sure to find out the details. Some hospitals are more amenable to tours than others, and a few have nominal per-person charges.

Classes, especially for new siblings, are also available.

Dates/Hours: Call the community relations department
                 of your local hospital for a tour
Admission: Varies
Phone: Check phone listing

105

Newspaper Publishers

Western Michigan's daily and weekly newspapers are happy to share their publishing processes with interested groups. Press runs are especially exciting for kids. Contact the following in advance to arrange a tour:

The Advance
2141 Port Sheldon Road, Jenison
669-2700

Battle Creek Enquirer
155 W. Van Buren
964-7161

Benton Harbor Herald-Palladium
3450 Hollywood, St. Joseph
429-2400

Grand Haven Tribune
101 N. 3rd
842-6400
Press runs 12–1 P.M.

Holland Sentinel
54 W. 8th Street
392-2311
Open houses for public. Group tours.

Kalamazoo Gazette
401 S. Burdick
345-3511
Groups of 10–20, 8 years old or older. Press runs 10:30–2 P.M.

Muskegon Chronicle
981 3rd Street
722-0300
Group tours

Trolley Car Tours and Rides

Have your children ever ridden a trolley car? Check these out:

Muskegon Trolley Company

They'll love touring Muskegon in one of three trolleys operated by the Muskegon Trolley Company. They run along two scenic routes with beaches, state parks, and an amusement center on the tours. Memorial Day–Labor Day, 11 A.M.–6 P.M. Departs from downtown Muskegon. Just $.25 per ride. Call 724-6420 for further information.

Harbor Trolley and Transit

Grand Haven's local transit system offers rides on demand to downtown and waterfront areas. It runs every day in the summer and offers half-hour narrated tours about area history and attractions. Memorial Day–Labor Day. Chinook Pier, 842-3200.

Ada

Amway Corporate Tours

Industrial displays, manufacturing exhibits, and audio/visual presentations trace the history of Amway to the present in a very well-done presentation.

For high school age or above, this one-hour walking tour is not recommended for young children. Groups must total ten or less.

Dates/Hours:	Four tours daily: 9 and 11 A.M., 1 and 3 P.M. Advance reservations required
Admission:	Free
Phone:	676-6701
Address:	I-96 east of Grand Rapids, Fulton Street exit, 4–5 miles east to 1575 E. Fulton, Ada

Augusta

Kellogg Farm Dairy Center

Either take the self-guided tour (follow the painted hoofs) or arrange a group tour around the Kellogg Farm Dairy Center. From Stop #1 (Meet the Cow) to Stop #8 (Environmental Concerns), state-of-the-art livestock care and handling is evident. Kids will especially enjoy the feed center, nursery, and milking parlor (midday milking at 12:30 P.M., lasts three hours).

The Kellogg Dairy Farm is part of Michigan State University's Biological Station, one of the largest in the U.S. The organization is dedicated to research and education, and 15,000 visit the farm annually.

Guided tours last one hour. Schedule a visit to the nearby Kellogg Bird Sanctuary on the same day!

Dates/Hours:	Visitor Center: Monday–Friday 8–5
	Self-guided tours: 8 A.M.–sunset, seven days a week
Admission:	Free; small charge for tour.
Phone:	671-2507. Group tours, call 671-2412
Address:	North on 40th Street from M-89 east of Gull Lake, 16 miles northeast of Kalamazoo

Battle Creek

Binder Park Zoo

Ride the ZO & O Railroad through the zoo's 18 exotic and 14 domestic animal exhibits, which present animals in their natural forest environments. The zoo runs numerous conservation programs to preserve several endangered species.

The Miller Children's Zoo includes a renowned dinosaur replica, domestic animal exhibits, and interactive hands-on displays for children.

Binder Park Zoo makes a nice day trip, with picnic shelters, a restaurant, and a gift shop on the grounds. It also offers a full calendar of events for children — nature walks, breakfasts with the animals, Zooper Summer Day Camp, overnight at the zoo, and Reptile Weekend are a few. (See also The Great Zoo Boo in "Seasonal Fun.")

Dates/Hours: Mid-April–mid-October: weekdays 9–5, Saturday 9–6, Sunday 11–6 June-August open until 8 P.M. on Wednesdays and Thursdays

Admission: Adults $4.50; ages 3–12 $2.50; under 2 free, seniors $3.50. Call for group rates

Phone: 979-1351

Address: I-94 to Exit 100 (Beadle Lake Road); three miles south of I-94 at 7400 Division

Bridgman

Cook Nuclear Plant

Visit Cook Energy Information Center at the Nuclear Plant to find out how energy is supplied now, and what we can expect in the year 2001 (that's not far off any more!).

Included at the center are three theater shows: a futuristic glimpse of energy production, a rotating model of the Cook plant, and a film tour showing what's behind the plant's closed doors. The colorful 45-minute musical presentation pleases kids.

The nature trail is also open.

Dates/Hours:	Closed Mondays and holidays; otherwise open 10–5
Admission:	Free
Phone:	465-5901
Address:	I-96 west to I-94 West, get off on exit 16 (Bridgman), and go 3½ miles north on Red Arrow Highway

Caledonia

Dairy Farms

Pleasant Acres Dairy Farm, located at 4091 100th SE, Caledonia, tel. 891-9944, provides tours for school groups and organizations. Call ahead to schedule.

Twin Pines Farms, located at 6990 100th SE, Caledonia, tel. 891-8257, gives tours for preschool and kindergarten groups. Call in January for spring tours.

Coloma

Deer Forest

Since the 1940s, Deer Forest has given thousands of children hands-on experiences with its gentlest animals (the monkeys and the two black bears are NOT among the touchable animals). Several hundred tame deer eat out of children's hands, as well as baby zebras, camels, and other baby animals. You'll have to see for yourself what an audad is. It's a very educational park.

Other activities include pony and camel rides, a restored carousel, a ferris wheel, kids' rides, tiny little-kid rides, and train rides. Kids might spend hours in the elaborate "Wild Child Play Habitat." There's also a shady park, picnic area, gift shop, and concessions.

"Santa's House and Reindeer" and "Halloween Week" are big hits, too!

Dates/Hours: Daily 10–6 Memorial Day–Labor Day
Admission: Adults $7; kids 3–11 $5; under 3 free. Rides $.75. Season passes available
Phone: 468-4961
Address: I-96 just north of Benton Harbor, Coloma exit 39. Two miles to 6800 Marquette

Gobles

Grandpa's Animal Farm

This popular attraction is located near the Kal-Haven Trail and the Michigan Fisheries Interpretive Center, and would make a good tie-in trip with either one.

The main attractions are the donkeys, horses, and goats. In the summer, bunnies, ducks, geese, pigs, and lambs are also big kid pleasers. The farm also has an 1830s-1850s log cabin with an open well, a nature trail, and a picnic area.

Many school groups visit, as do tent campers and Kal-Haven bikers/hikers.

Dates/Hours: Self-guided tour. Open year-round;
closed Mondays
Admission: Adults $2.50; children $2.
Special rates for groups
Phone: 628-2854
Address: 2½ miles east of Gobles on
County Road 388

TOURS AND EXCURSIONS

115

Blandford Nature Center

Naturalist Laurie Rosenberg will guide groups of ten or more lower-elementary students through any of the Nature Center's 143 acres of marshes, ravines, fields, and forests, tailoring her tour to each group's age level and special interests.

Register for fall tours beginning in August, for spring tours in January. They are in great demand — spring tours are usually filled by March.

If you chaperone a class field trip, try to arrange child care for your other children. Then you'll be able to devote full attention to the class and your touring child.

Your family may opt for a self-guided tour. Sign in at the Visitor Center, grab a map, and spend an hour or two hiking on one of the many marked trails. Short trails are great for the toddler crowd!

Dates/Hours: Tours by arrangement. Self-guided tours Monday–Friday 9–5; Saturday–Sunday 1–5
Admission: Tours $1 per student
Phone: 453-6192
Address: 1715 Hillburn NW, north off Leonard in Grand Rapids

Grand Rapids

Fish Ladder

In the fall, bystanders flock to the Grand River and Sixth Street Dam to watch the salmon fight their way up the salmon ladder to spawn. The viewing area is actually a unique sculpture by local artist Joseph Kinnebrew.

Be sure to dress for the weather. Preschoolers seem to get especially cold on fall days when they're near water.

Dates/Hours: Any fall day
Admission: Free
Address: West bank of the Grand River at Sixth
            Street Dam, near downtown Grand Rapids

Grand Rapids

John Ball Park and Zoo

It's no surprise that the children's petting zoo is always a favorite part of our kids' zoo visits — especially when the goats begin nibbling on shoelaces! The monkeys and otters also rate extra attention, and the snakes create their own brand of excitement.

A picnic area and duck pond are located just outside the zoo entrance.

The zoo schedules activities and displays for holidays and special occasions and for Community Enrichment Day (see "Educational Activities"). A new aquarium will open in 1995.

Teens (ages 14–18) may volunteer at the zoo. Your family may adopt one or more zoo animals and take gifts for them (bananas, apples, carrots, kennels, blankets, and food dishes).

Dates/Hours:	Open year-round 10–4. Summer hours 10–6
Admission:	Adults $3; children 5–13 and seniors $1.50; 4 and under free
Phone:	336-3684
Address:	U.S. 131 to downtown Market Street exit, left to Fulton, $2\frac{1}{2}$ miles

Grand Haven

Grand Rapids City Water Filtration Plant

There's a lot more to clean water than meets the eye (or nose)! Children will find out firsthand how complex water treatment really is — when they see the plant's water filters, settling basins, laboratories, and large equipment that pumps water through Grand Rapids.

The plant staff can handle tours of up to 60 people, and has no age limits. The tour lasts $1\frac{1}{2}$-2 hours, depending on the curiosity level of your group.

Dates/Hours:	By arrangement
Admission:	Free
Phone:	456-3700, call two weeks ahead for reservation
Address:	Approximately 7 miles south of Grand Haven at 17350 Lake Michigan Drive (near Lakeshore Drive)

Grand Rapids

Gypsum Mine Tour

Hike in and find out how gypsum is mined and learn about this mine's history. Gypsum is used for mineral collections and by local businesses for coal.

Dates/Hours:	Tuesday–Friday by appointment
Admission:	Adults $2; elementary students $1.25
	Minimum $30 for groups
Phone:	241-1619
Address:	1200 Judd SW, Grand Rapids

Grand Rapids

Kent County International Airport

Conducted by a police officer, airport tours include stops at security checkpoints, baggage claim areas, and the fire station. This tour is especially popular with lower-elementary students, although 50 year olds have requested tours, too! The tour takes 1–1½ hours.

You don't need an official tour group to visit the airport, though. Go upstairs to the observatory at the airport's main terminal for a great view of plane takeoffs and landings. Preschoolers love to watch airport workers fueling and signaling the planes, handling baggage, and driving those important little scooters.

Get a closer look at the planes and their impressive sounds from the outdoor viewing/picnic area on Kraft Avenue. Bring a picnic lunch!

Dates/Hours:	Self-tours any time; the airport's busiest time is 4:30 P.M. every day
Admission:	Free
Phone:	336-4548; call well in advance to reserve a group tour
Address:	5500 44th Street SE. Outdoor viewing area is north off 52nd Street on Kraft Avenue

Grand Rapids

Voigt House Victorian Museum

Owned by the Grand Rapids Public Museum, the Voigt House is a chateau-style mansion built in 1895, with furnishings from the 1800s. Special exhibits are shown periodically. All collections belong to the Voigt family.

- Guided tours for 3rd–5th-graders
- Architectural tours for junior high students
- Docents/volunteers may be as young as 12 years old
- Christmas program in November–December

We recommend only a quick trip through for younger children, especially if they are like ours — busy every minute, and potentially very fast.

Dates/Hours:	Tuesdays 11–3. Second and fourth Sunday of the month 1–3
Admission:	Adults $3; children 6–12 and seniors $2
Phone:	456-4600
Address:	115 College Avenue SE, Heritage Hill area of Grand Rapids

Hart

Mac Wood's Dune Rides

The great Silver Lake sand dunes provide a wonderful testament to nature's handiwork. The eight-mile dune ride is exciting, informative, and lasts about 40 minutes.

It gets bouncy at times, so hang on to your hats and kids. Sunglasses and cameras are advised.

Schedule groups in advance.

Dates/Hours: Mid-May–Labor Day; 9:30–dusk
May/June/September: shorter hours, closed Thursday
Admission: Adults $9; 11 and under $6
Phone: 873-2817
Address: U.S. 31 to Shelby or Hart exits, 10 miles west at Silver Lake

Holland

Brooks Beverages Plant

Take a self-guided tour of a soft-drink bottling factory. Watch from the observation deck as a heavy syrup is turned into a store-ready product, and bottles are filled on running conveyor lines with your favorite soft-drink brands.

The tour is appropriate for lower elementary through high school students.

Dates/Hours: Monday–Friday 8:30–5; call for
                reservations
Admission: Free
Phone: 396-1281
Address: 777 Brooks Avenue, Holland

Holland

DeKlomp Wooden Shoe and Delftware Factory

Take a self-guided factory tour and talk with Dutch crafts-men as they carve wooden shoes by hand and machine. Watch artists pour, handpaint, and fire the famous blue-and-white delftware at the only delft-pottery factory in the U.S. A large retail store has plenty of souvenirs for you to take home.

Holland's one and only tulip farm, Veldheer's, is also located here. Veldheer's grows more than 160 varieties of tulips with *two million* blooms in season. During the sum-mer, visitors' cameras capture photos of thousands of peo-nies, daylilies, irises, and Dutch lillies.

Dates/Hours:	Gardens: April–October, Monday–Friday 8–6, Saturday–Sunday 9–5. Factory open year-round
Admission:	Gardens: adults $2.50; 16 and under $1 Factory: free
Phone:	399-1803
Address:	12755 Quincy. On U.S. 31, 2 miles north of Holland

Holland

Dutch Village

This is one of Holland's best attractions for kids! Century-old Dutch lifestyles are recreated in seasonal gardens, Dutch cuisine, *klompen* dances, and scenic architecture, bridges, and canals. Children will love riding the restored carousel and huge swing.

Peek into the farmhouse and barn (with a petting zoo), museum, weigh house, and wooden shoe factory. Dutch Village also features several fine import shops — you won't be able to resist opening your wallet.

Dutch Village is sandwiched between U.S. 31 and Outlets of Holland, but once inside, you will hardly notice the outside road traffic.

Dates/Hours:	Late April–September 1: Monday–Thursday 9:30–5:30; Friday–Saturday 9:30–7:30; closed Sunday
Admission:	Shops are free. Admission to remainder: adults $5; children $3
Phone:	396-1475
Address:	U.S. 31 at James Street, Holland

Holland

Windmill Island

"DeZwaan" is a 200-year-old windmill from Zwaan, Netherlands, brought to the U.S. about 15 years ago. It is the central feature of the 30-acre Windmill Island Municipal Park, which also includes a drawbridge, thousands of in-season flowers, a carousel, and carefully replicated Dutch buildings. Kids love the "Little Netherlands," a mechanized miniature Dutch village.

Tour guides in traditional costume explain the windmill's operation and importance in Dutch history. Other educational features include a video about windmills and old-time *klompen* dance. Ride the old Dutch carousel, and check out the souvenirs and concessions. You may opt to bring your own picnic.

The windmill tour lasts 20 minutes, but plan on two hours to see it all.

Dates/Hours: May–October: Monday–Saturday 9–6,
              Sunday open at 11:30 A.M.
Admission: Adults $5; children 5–12 years $2.50
Phone: 396-5433
Address: Corner of 7th and Lincoln Avenue,
              Holland

TOURS AND EXCURSIONS

Holland

Wooden Shoe Factory

Watch 100-year-old machinery and highly skilled hand carving turn blocks of wood into *klompen,* or wooden shoes. The Wooden Shoe Factory is the only one of its kind in North America.

The gift shop offers many wooden toys and souvenirs. The Country Store imports cheese, chocolates, and other delicacies.

Dates/Hours:	Monday–Saturday 8–4:30, extended hours during Tulip Time Festival
Admission:	$.25; children 5 and under are free
Phone:	396-6513
Address:	447 U.S. 31 at 16th Street, Holland

Kalamazoo

Michigan Fisheries Interpretive Center

During some years, over 100 million walleyes hatch at the Wolf Lake State Fish Hatchery. The Fish Hatchery supplies hundreds of Michigan's public access lakes, rivers, and streams with salmon, trout, pike, sturgeon, and muskies.

Guides will take visitors through the Fisheries Interpretive Center and parts of the Fish Hatchery. In addition to viewing ALL those fish, kids will love seeking out the two old giant sturgeon swimming along the bottom of the "show pond." They'll also be able to feed the trout!

Fish threats are described in the Interpretive Center, notably alewives and lamprey (the ones with sucker-like mouths loaded with teeth!).

Dates/Hours:	Year-round: Wednesday–Saturday 10–5
	Memorial Day–November 15: Also
	Sunday 12–5
Admission:	Free
Phone:	668-2876
Address:	US 131 to Exit 38B (M-43) six miles to
	Fish Hatchery Road. Turn left, second
	drive

TOURS AND EXCURSIONS

Kalamazoo

Train Barn

The Train Barn, a wonderfully cared-for train museum and hobby shop, has been featured on national television and in several regional and national magazine articles.

The whole upstairs is a 2,800 square-foot Lionel train layout; it is open only on Saturdays and is always crowded. The main floor is divided into a museum and hobby shop. The museum showcases antique and modern collectible trains of all sizes.

While kids enjoy the Train Barn, nostalgic adults love it! Warning: There are no restrooms in the building.

Dates/Hours: Tuesday–Friday 4–9, Saturday 10–5
(upstairs open 11–4:30). Open other
assorted days
Admission: Main floor museum free.
Upstairs: adults $1; kids $.50
Phone: 327-4016
Address: I-94 to Sprinkle Road exit. $6\frac{1}{2}$ miles
south to Nash. Turn west, $\frac{1}{2}$ mile to East
Shore, $\frac{1}{2}$ mile further

Lowell

James C. Veen Observatory

For an uplifting family activity, spend an evening searching for stars and planets at James C. Veen Observatory. Find Jupiter in the early season, and Saturn (and its famous rings) in late summer and fall.

Owned and operated by members of the Grand Rapids Amateur Astronomical Association, the observatory boasts two powerful telescopes and a turning roof. Volunteers will gladly assist in your star search.

Guests are invited to twice-monthly open houses from April to October, if the sky is clear. GRAAA also hosts a one-week open house in mid-August, regardless of sky conditions, from 8:30 to 11 P.M. Bring bug repellent on summer visits! The group also welcomes new members to its junior astronomers' division.

Dates/Hours:	Second Saturday and last Friday of each month, April–October. April, September, and October: 8:30–11 P.M.
Admission:	Adults $1.50; children under 12 $.50
Phone:	897-7065; or Chaffee Planetarium, 456-3977
Address:	3308 Kissing Rock SE, Lowell

Portage

Celery Flats Interpretive Center

Who would think that celery could be interesting, and just plain fun? The Celery Flats Interpretive Center provides a 3-D look at Kalamazoo's history as the country's greatest celery producer with a tour of its greenhouses, celery gardens, and photos of real farm families. Retired celery farmers serving as weekend guides provide nitty-gritty details from their perspective.

After your visit inside, picnic and play in the surrounding park, walk the two-mile nature trail, or take a 45-minute canoe trip from a dropoff point on Portage Creek back to the Center (cost: $6 for two people). Last, plan to stop at the one-room schoolhouse and grain elevator across the street.

Dates/Hours: May to mid-September, Friday 12–5,
              Saturday 10–5, Sunday 1–5
Admission: Adults $2; children 5–15 $1
Phone: 329-4522
Address: I-94 to Exit 76A (S. Westnedge), south 2
              miles, east to Garden Lane

132

Rockford

Hush Puppy Shoes at Wolverine Worldwide

Tour the shoe production plant at Wolverine Worldwide. In a half an hour, you will glimpse the whole process, from heat steam and pressure areas to the assembly line. Shoes are cut and soles are made here.

This plant produces 31,000-32,000 pairs of Hush Puppies each year, and ships many thousands of shoe soles all over the world.

Dates/Hours: Call to schedule tour
Admission: Free
Phone: 866-5514
Address: 9341 Courtland, Rockford

Saugatuck

Dune Rides

Thirty-five-minute scenic rides through Lake Michigan's sand dunes, woodlands, and Goshorn Lake promise pure excitement for kids.

Dune Schooners can seat up to 20 people, and are driven by experienced driver-guides. They do have a tendency to make the ride more "exciting" than just driving a car down the street.

Dates/Hours: May 1–September 30. Monday–Saturday 10–6, Sunday 12–6. July–August: Open until 8 P.M.

Admission: Adults $7.50, children 10 and under $4.50

Phone: 857-2253

Address: I-196 to exit 41 north of Saugatuck. West ½ mile on Blue Star Highway

Saugatuck

SS *Keewatin* Ship Museum

Located in Saugatuck's colorful Harbour Village, this 336-foot Great Lakes steamship is permanently docked as a nautical museum, complete with tour guides. Beginning in 1908, the *Keewatin* took passengers for long luxury cruises of the Great Lakes. It burned 150 tons of coal per week!

Other Harbour Village attractions include boat cruises with fun-sounding themes, perch fishing trips, a gift shop, and a patio bar.

In fact, Harbour Village has a special tour package for groups of 35 or more: a tour of the SS *Keewatin,* a narrated cruise aboard the *City of Douglas,* and lunch for $17.95 takes about three hours. Or do the SS *Keewatin* tour and narrated cruise for $10.95.

Dates/Hours: Memorial–Labor Day: 10–4:30, tours on the half hour
Admission: Museum: adults $3; children 6–12 years $1.50; 5 and under free
Phone: 857-2107
Address: Blue Star Highway to Union in Douglas, north to Harbour Village, south bank of Kalamazoo Lake

THE GREAT OUTDOORS

Great Beaches

Children of all age groups enjoy trips to the beach — some to eat sand, others to swim, and still others to watch girls (and guys). Bring sunscreen, picnics, beach toys, and make a summer memory or two!

State Park Beaches

Augusta: Fort Custer
Grand Haven: Grand Haven
Holland: Holland/Saugatuck Dunes
Ionia: Ionia
Mears: Silver Lake
Middleville: Yankee Springs
Muskegon: P. J. Hoffmaster,
   Muskegon State Park
North Muskegon: Duck Lake
Pentwater: Charles Mears
South Haven: Van Buren
Sawyer: Warren Dunes

Area County and City Beaches

Allegan area

Dumont Lake
Most popular in the area; great beach and playground

Gun Lake
Large inland lake, nice small swimming beach, playground

Littlejohn Lake
New and modern park, sandy beach with concessions

West Side Park
On Lake Michigan — beach, playground, great for reunions

Battle Creek

Willard Beach and Park 966-3431
George B. Place, 2 miles south on Goguac lake

Grand Rapids area

Hilton Park–Green Lake 891-1803
Great family lake, park, and beach

Long Lake
17 Mile Road and Long Lake Drive
Bath house, fishing, picnic areas, playground

Meyers Lake
M-44 (Belding Road) to Meyers Lake Avenue, turn north. Turn right just before 12 Mile.
Bath house, fishing, picnic area, playground, tennis courts

Wabasis Lake
M-44 (Belding Road) to Wabasis Avenue, turn north. Park is on Wabasis Avenue.
Bath house, campgrounds, fishing, nature trails, picnic area, playground.

Holland area

Grose Park
Crockery Lake — swimming beach, playground, peaceful atmosphere

Kirk Park
On Lake Michigan — beach, wooded sand dunes — a perfect spot for the day

Tunnel Park
A beautiful Lake Michigan beach — popular for sunbathing — great children's play area

Kalamazoo Area

Prairie View Park
East of US-131 on U Avenue between Portage and Oakridge
Swimming beach and bath house — a great family beach

Coldbrook Park
South of I-94 on MN Avenue, eight miles east of Kalamazoo
Swimming beach and bath house — good spot for camping and boating

Maple Glen
Westnedge Avenue — close to Kalamazoo River, Kalamazoo Nature Center, and downtown Kalamazoo.
New park to open in 1994 with swimming beach

THE GREAT OUTDOORS

141

Bronson Park
Business 31 to Sherman Boulevard (west) to park

Lake Harbor Park
US-31 to Pontaluna Road (west) to Lake Harbor

Lakeside Beach
Swimming, fishing; sandy beach with lifeguard

North Shore
North Shore Drive
A great beach with dune climb next to Lake Michigan shore

Medbury Park
US-31 N to Colby/Whitehall exit to Old Channel Trail (west) to park.

Meinert County Park
Business 31 to Whitehall (north) to Meinert (west)

Pere Marquette Park
Business 31 to Sherman (west)

Pioneer City Park
US-31, take M-120/ North Muskegon exit (west) to Whitehall Road (north) to Giles Road (west); north on Scenic Drive

142

Saugatuck

Oval Beach
US-31 Blue Star Highway to Union — right on
Perryman

Douglas Park
Lakeshore Drive south of Oval Beach

Western Michigan has many parks, all different sizes, dedicated to a variety of activities. Following is a sampling; city and county parks departments can provide information, brochures, and maps.

Call before visiting to be sure your chosen activities are still offered — budgets, acts of God, and other circumstances may change their availability. Check for information about lifeguards at the beaches you expect to visit. Also, as indicated, most parks have toilet facilities or restrooms; most are modern, but a few are primitive.

Amenities Key

A	Boat Launch	M	Open Shelter
B	Ball Diamonds	N	Picnicking
C	Bath House	O	Playground
D	Bike Trails	P	Shelter House
E	Campgrounds	Q	Soccer
F	Cross Country Skiing	R	Swimming
G	Exercise Trails	S	Tennis Courts
H	Fishing	T	Winter Sports
I	Frisbee Golf	U	Basketball
J	Golf Course	V	Restrooms
K	Hiking/Walking	W	Beach
L	Nature Trails	X	Lake Michigan Access

Allegan

Name: **Dumont Lake, Allegan**
Address: 33rd Street, north of 112nd Avenue
Acreage: 19
Amenities: AMNOSVW

Name: **Gun Lake, Shelbyville**
Address: Corner of Patterson and 124th
Acreage: 4
Amenities: ANORSVW

Name: **Littlejohn, Allegan**
Address: 113th Avenue, west of 34th
Acreage: 113
Amenities: BCMNRSUVW

Name: **Silver Creek, Hamilton**
Address: 134th Avenue, east of M-40 north
Acreage: 320
Amenities: ENOV
Comments horse trail

Name: **West Side, Fennville**
Address: Lakeshore Road, south of M-89
Acreage: 11
Amenities: ANOVX

Battle Creek

Name: **Binder Park Golf Course**
Address: 6723 B Drive, south
Phone   966-3431
Acreage: 650
Amenities: FJV (except winter)

Name: **Fell Park**
Address: North end of Park Ridge Drive
Phone   966-3431
Acreage: 80
Amenities: BDKNOPSV

Name: **Fort Custer Recreation Area**
Address: 15501 Dickman Road
Phone   731-4200
Acreage: 3,000
Amenities: AEFHKLNORV

Name: **John Bailey Park**
Address: 1392 Capital Avenue NE
Phone   966-3431
Acreage: 80
Amenities: BHKMNOV

Name: **Kellogg Forest**
Address: 42nd Street, Augusta
Phone   731-4597
Acreage: 700
Amenities: FHKLNV
Comments: research

Name:	**Kimball Pine Park**
Address:	1150 E. Michigan
Phone	784-0815
Acreage:	60
Amenities:	GKMNO

Name:	**Linear Park Pathway**
Address:	Many access points in Battle Creek
Phone	966-3431
Acreage:	16 miles
Amenities:	DFHKMNO
Comments:	by river

Name:	**Spring Lake**
Address:	Northwest corner of North and Emmett
Phone	966-3431
Acreage:	53
Amenities:	HKLNO
Comments:	duck lagoon

Name:	**Willard Beach**
Address:	George B Pl., off Capital SW
Phone	966-3431
Acreage:	16
Amenities:	HNORVW

Name: **Coldbrook Park**
Address: MN Avenue, south of I-94, east of Kalamazoo.
Acreage: 210
Amenities: BCEFHKLMNORW

Name: **Maple Glen Park**
Address: Westnedge, just north of G Avenue
Acreage: 180
Amenities: BKLM
Comments will grow

Name: **Prairie View Park**
Address: East of U.S. 131, U Avenue
Acreage: 210
Amenities: ABCFHKLMNORTW

Name: **River Oaks Park**
Address: On Morrow Lake off M-96
Acreage: 200
Amenities: ABHKLNOP

Name: **Scotts Mill Park**
Address: Q Avenue at 35th Street
Acreage: 200
Amenities: BHLMNO
Comments: grist mill

Kalamazoo (city of)

Name: **Milham Park**
Address: Kilgore at Milham
Acreage: 139
Amenities: BLNOV

Name: **Spring Valley**
Address: 2600 Mt. Olivet
Acreage: 196
Amenities: BLNOQUV

Kent County

Name: **Fallasburg Park**
Address: Covered Bridge and Fallasburg Park Drives
Acreage: 458
Amenities: BHLMNOPTV

Name: **John Ball Park and Zoo**
Address: Fulton NW
Acreage: 104
Amenities: BNOSV

Name: **Johnson Park**
Address: Wilson and Butterworth
Acreage: 245
Amenities: BDGHIKNOPTV

Name: **Lamoreaux Park**
Address: Coit and Bailey
Acreage: 249
Amenities: BEFHKLNT

Name: **Palmer Park**
Address: Clyde Park between 44th and 52nd
Acreage: 340
Amenities: BDFHJKLNOTV

Name: **Pickerel Lake**
Address: Ramsdell south of M-44
Acreage: 235
Amenities: FHKLV

Name: **Seidman Park**
Address: Honey Creek and Leonard
Acreage: 422
Amenities: FHKLMTV

Name: **Townsend Park**
Address: Cannonsburg and Ramsdell
Acreage: 157
Amenities: BFHKLMNOPYTV

Name: **Walker Park**
Address: 84th Street, west of Clyde Park
Acreage: 62
Amenities: BDKNOPQTV

Muskegon County

Name: **Blue Lake**
Address: Nichols Road
Acreage: 25
Amenities: AEHNOV

Name:	**Meinert Park**
Address:	Whitehall Road to Meinert Park Road
Acreage:	50
Amenities:	NOVWX

Name:	**Moore Park**
Address:	Half Moon Lake M-37, north of M-46
Acreage:	25
Amenities:	ABHNRV

Name:	**Patterson Park**
Address:	South of Ravenna
Acreage:	20
Amenities:	NOV

Name:	**Pioneer Park**
Address:	1563 Scenic Drive
Acreage:	145
Amenities:	BENOPSUV

Name:	**Twin Lakes Park**
Address:	M-120 to Blue Lake Road, Twin Lake
Acreage:	10
Amenities:	AHNORUVW

Name:	**Wolf Lake**
Address:	Apple Avenue to Wolf Lake, north
Acreage:	6
Amenities:	HNORUVW

Name: **Kruse Park (formerly Bronson)**
Address: Sherman Boulevard and Beach/724-6704
Acreage: 80
Amenities: BHKLNOPX

Name: **McGraft Park**
Address: 2204 Wickham Drive/724-6704
Acreage: 91
Amenities: BFHKLNOSU

Name: **Pere Marquette Park**
Address: Beach Street on Lake Michigan
Phone: 724-6704
Acreage: 32
Amenities: HNOX

Name: **Ross Park**
Address: Randall and Wellesley, Norton Shores
Phone: 798-4391
Acreage: 43
Amenities: ABCGILMNORSUVW

Name: **Lake Harbor**
Address: Lake Harbor Road, Norton Shores
Phone: 798-4391
Acreage: 77
Amenities: HKLMNRVWX

Name: **Kirk Park**
Address: Lakeshore Drive
Acreage: 66
Amenities: KNPRWX

Name: **Tunnel Park**
Address: Lakeshore Drive, Holland
Acreage: 22.5
Amenities: NORWX

Name: **Pigeon Creek Park**
Address: Stanton, Olive Township
Acreage: 282
Amenities: FKN

Name: **North Beach Park**
Address: North Shore Drive, Ferrysburg
Acreage: 20
Amenities: NRX

Name: **Riverside Park**
Address: North Cedar, Robins Township
Acreage: 50
Amenities: AHNP

Name: **Deer Creek**
Address: 60th Avenue, off Leonard, Eastmanville
Acreage: 2.5
Amenities: AHN

THE GREAT OUTDOORS

153

Name: **Grose Park**
Address: Crockery Lake, Chester Township
Acreage: 40
Amenities: BNORW

Name: **Hager Park**
Address: 28th Street, Bauer
Acreage: 104
Amenities: BLNOP

Name: **Spring Grove Park**
Address: Greenly Street, Hudsonville
Acreage: 16
Amenities: BNO

Other Wonderful Parks

Name: **Ada Township Park**
Address: Buttrick Drive SE
Phone   676-0520
Acreage: 57
Amenities: BFHKLMNOSV

Name: **Kindleberger Park**
Address: Parchment
Phone   349-3785
Acreage: 40
Amenities: BV

Name: **Ramona Park**
Address: Portage
Phone   329-4522
Acreage: 67
Amenities: BCHNOPQRSUVW

Augusta

Fort Custer Recreation Area

Three thousand acres of beauty with four lakes and high rolling meadows are located between the Kalamazoo River and the state military training site.

In addition to acclaimed hiking and cross-country ski trails, Fort Custer offers fishing, swimming, boating, horseback-riding trails, playground and picnic areas, and modern camping facilities.

The International Hot Air Balloon Festival draws campers from all over the map every Fourth of July weekend (see "Festivals").

Dates/Hours: Weekdays 8–4:30, weekends 8–7:30
Admission: State park sticker: Seasonal $18, daily $4
Phone: 731-4200
Address: I-94 to exit 95 (Helmer Road). North to
M-96, turn left. Seven miles to park
entrance, W. Dickman Road

THE GREAT OUTDOORS

155

Augusta

Kellogg Bird Sanctuary and Kellogg Forest

Walk on the W. K. Kellogg Biological Station's self-guided trails through a bird sanctuary and forest, where hundreds of wild birds — ducks, geese, swans, and birds of prey — migrate through and live. Children will love hand-feeding the waterfowl.

The bird sanctuary is especially active during spring and fall: spring is an important nesting season, and three major migratory routes cross at the sanctuary.

Located on Wintergreen Lake, the Kellogg Bird Sanctuary is nationally known for wildlife management and environmental education programs. The sanctuary hosts over 250,000 visitors annually.

The beautiful forest, located nearby, contains hundreds of experimental tree varieties.

Dates/Hours:	May–October 9 A.M.–dusk, November–April 9–5
Admission:	Sanctuary: adults $2; children 4–12 $.50; 3 and under free
Phone:	671-2510
Address:	Two miles north off M-89 on 40th to C Avenue. Kellogg Forest is nearby

Battle Creek

Leila Arboretum

Over 600 labeled varieties of trees and flowers can be found in this arboretum, as well as an 80-acre English landscape garden containing an exceptional collection of sun and shade perennial flower beds.

The Kingman Museum of Natural History is located on the premises as well (see "Educational Activities").

Dates/Hours: Always open
Admission: Free
Phone: 969-0270
Address: W. Michigan Avenue at 20th,
              Battle Creek

Belmont

Grand Rogue Campgrounds, Canoe and Tube Livery

Tubing is safe and fun, even for young children. Float down the Rogue River and enjoy nature on an inflatable raft equipped with paddles (the Livery staff will drive you to a launching spot upriver from the Grand Rogue Campgrounds).

Two-hour canoe trips on the Grand River begin at the Knapp Street Bridge. Four-hour trips begin at the Ada Covered Bridge. A maximum of three people to a canoe is allowed.

Many family activities, including hayrides, are available at this Belmont resort, which includes 75 wooded acres with a great swimming and fishing lake. Golf is nearby.

Visitors flock to the campgrounds for historical wartime reenactments (see "Educational Activities").

Dates/Hours:	All year, weather permitting
Admission:	Tubes: 1- or 2-hour trips $3/hour per tube. Canoes: 2-hour trips $18; 4-hour trips $22
Phone:	361-1053
Address:	6400 West River Drive, Belmont (west of East Beltline)

THE GREAT OUTDOORS

158

Cedar Springs

Howard Christensen Nature Center

Study a variety of animal habitats at this Kent City nature preserve. With five miles of trails, lakes, and ponds, Christensen Nature Center is great for family hiking and cross-country skiing. Fall colors and spring wildflowers are especially inviting.

Guided tours are available for school groups, and learning stations and classes make nature study and environmental education easy.

Toilet facilities are available.

Dates/Hours: Open year-round. Monday–Friday 8–4, trails open 7 days. Tours and classes by arrangement
Admission: Free
Phone: 887-1852
Address: U.S. 131 to Cedar Springs exit, west on M-46, north on Red Pine, west on 18 Mile Road, right back on Red Pine

THE GREAT OUTDOORS

Blandford Nature Center

Walk or cross-country ski on 143 acres of marked nature trails. The Visitor Center has hands-on collections, a wild animal hospital, a one-room schoolhouse, and outdoor living enclosures for disabled animals.

One-day classes, such as Earth Tales, Bear's Autumn Picnic, Knee-High Naturalist, and Birdfeeding Weekend, are geared to various age groups. They are very popular, so call early for topics and registration. See "Seasonal Fun" for Blandford's spring tree tapping demonstrations.

Dates/Hours:	Monday–Friday 9–5, Saturday–Sunday 1–5
Admission:	Free; donations welcome. Guided tours $1.25 per person in advance. Small fee for classes.
Phone:	453-6192
Address:	U.S. 131 to Leonard St. exit, $3\frac{1}{2}$ miles west to Hillburn, then north to end

THE GREAT OUTDOORS

Grand Rapids

Michigan Botanic Garden

Opening in January 1995, the Michigan Botanic Garden will feature a children's garden, entryway atrium, formal gardens, and the state's largest public conservatory, with classrooms, a library, a meeting center, a restaurant, and a gift shop. Hands-on learning for all ages will be emphasized at the conservatory.

The botanic garden will emphasize the natural look, with prairies, marshes, and perennial gardens. Two pond gardens should also appeal to the kids. Also, look for theme gardens, bridges, and walkways.

Funding for the $13.8 million botanic garden came from corporate and individual donations in an unprecedented display of community support. You must see this place as soon you can possibly get there!

Dates/Hours: Beginning January 1995, open all year
Admission: $2–$3
Phone: 957-1580
Address: Bradford Avenue, just off East Beltline north of I-96, Grand Rapids

THE GREAT OUTDOORS

Holland

DeGraaf Nature Center

With just 15.4 acres, DeGraaf Nature Center staff and volunteers have been able to provide a study of every biotic community: wetlands, ponds, creeks, meadows, and woodlands.

Boardwalks, woodchip trails, and benches allow for (almost) effortless walking. Habitats are filled with critters, and a butterfly garden is located near the Brower Interpretive Center. Be sure to get a look at the perennial and herb gardens. A log cabin and auditorium are also located on the grounds.

Weekly and monthly special events and classes attract children and adults: Maple Sugaring in March; Baby Animal Day in April; Butterfly Day in August; and Pioneer Christmas in December.

Dates/Hours: Trails: Dawn to dusk. Interpretive Center: Tuesday–Friday 12–4:30, weekends 2–4
Admission: Free
Phone: 396-2739
Address: U.S. 31 to Holland, west on 32nd Street, north on Graafschap to nature center

Kalamazoo

Al Sabo Nature Preserve

Nature preserves are different from parks. They exist to allow animal species to live in natural habitats, and for people to enjoy nature in beautiful, quiet settings. Parks are intensely managed to handle large numbers of people in a variety of activities.

Al Sabo Nature Preserve had to close to repair damage due to overuse, and just reopened in March, 1994. Its beautiful 750 acres hosts a number of endangered species. Officials ask that visitors be very considerate of the flora and fauna, stay on marked trails, and do NOT light bonfires. Use this and any nature preserve "quietly."

Warning: The preserve does not have restrooms.

Dates/Hours:	Daylight hours. Sometimes closed during spring and fall to avoid soil damage
Admission:	Free
Phone:	337-8755
Address:	Off Texas Drive immediately north of Rota Kiwan Scout Camp entrance

THE GREAT OUTDOORS

163

Kalamazoo

Kalamazoo Nature Center

Kalamazoo Nature Center is considered one of the top three nature centers in the U.S., serving over 140,000 people each year. Eight miles of walking trails wind through the center's 1,000 acres. Great care has been taken with the botanical gardens, arboretum, and interpretive center, which features animal exhibits, hands-on learning, and games.

Four or five naturalists serve on the permanent staff, and the education department has a full schedule of seasonal activities (such as maple sugaring and a harvest festival), camps, family programs, workshops, outreach programs, and classes! Most are offered on a first-come, first-served basis, although a few programs require pre-registration.

The research department is staffed by avian researchers, including the internationally known and respected director Raymond Adams.

Dates/Hours: Monday–Saturday 9–5, Sunday 1–5
Admission: Free for members. Nonmember adults
            $3; children $1.50;
            under 3 free
Phone: 381-1574
Address: U.S. 131 north of Kalamazoo to D
            Avenue exit, 2 miles east to 7000 N.
            Westnedge

E. Genevieve Gillette Nature Center

The star of Gillette Nature Center's show is our Lake Michigan sand dunes. A dune lookout, slide shows, exhibits, hikes, and a series of summer activities highlight the dunes' beauty and wildlife. Self-guided tours and special events for school groups are available.

Gillette Nature Center is located on Lake Michigan at nature-filled Hoffmaster State Park. The park also features a Dune Climb stairway to the beach, 11 miles of hiking trails, horseback-riding trails, picnic areas, and 333 campsites.

The Trillium Festival and Great Spangled Butterfly Days are held at the Nature Center too (see "Festivals").

Dates/Hours: Memorial–Labor Day: Tuesday–Sunday
9–5. Winter: Tuesday–Friday 1–5,
Saturday–Sunday 10–5
Admission: Daily State Park fee $4 per car; annual
$18 for all state park areas
Phone: 798-3573
Address: U.S. 31, 6 miles south of Muskegon to
Pontaluna Road exit. Six miles west to
6585 Lake Harbor

THE GREAT OUTDOORS

165

Parnell

Saul Lake Bog Nature Preserve

Saul Lake Bog is a perfect place for nature study because it maintains very delicate ecological balances. The Nature Preserve consists of 125 acres of woodlands, old agricultural fields, hardwood swamps, and the 55-acre bog. Several marked trails loop around the bog and habitat areas.

The area is perfect for bird watchers and for quiet enjoyment. Because it is very important to preserve the bog's natural state, do NOT disturb the wildlife — maintain a good distance from animals and birds. And don't bring pets.

Warning: The preserve does not have restrooms.

Dates/Hours: 7 A.M.–sunset year-round

Admission: Free

Address: Northeast of Grand Rapids. Take East Beltline to Cannonsburg Road, which turns into 5 Mile. Take 5 Mile to just past Parnell. North one mile on Gavin Lake Road to 6 Mile Road. Turn west, $\frac{1}{8}$ mile to gravel drive, go north to preserve; no sign on road

Saugatuck Dunes State Park

The beach area at Saugatuck Dunes State Park is remotely located and very private. It's a long hike from the parking lot, but gorgeous lake views from the top of the dunes make it all worthwhile.

This is probably not a good place to drag strollers, diaper bags, or playpens. It's just too far to walk with more than a towel, beach toys, and a cooler.

Dates/Hours: Daily 8 A.M.–10 P.M.
Admission: State park sticker: $4/car/day;
              $18 annually
Phone: 399-9390
Address: Blue Star Highway. 3 miles north of
              Saugatuck to 64th Street, 1½ miles to
              138th Avenue, 1 mile west

THE GREAT OUTDOORS

167

South Haven

Wicks Park and Boardwalk

With a lovely view over the Kalamazoo River and across to the old cottages, this is a peaceful park set away from summer tourist traffic, and a great picnic spot.

The boardwalk extends north to the chain ferry and south to the marina. It's busy at these ends, but the kids may enjoy the boat hustle-bustle.

Art lessons and ballroom dancing are offered at Wicks Park for a low $5 price. The park is often a setting for music concerts, too.

Dates/Hours: Anytime
Admission: Free
Phone: 857-5801
Address: Water and Main, South Haven

SEASONAL FUN

Spring

Caledonia

Hopping Down the Bunny Trail

Visit the Soper's Bunny Farm in the spring to see the baby bunnies, or to bring one home for a pet. We've found them to be easy-to-care-for pets.

Dates/Hours: Monday–Saturday 9–7
Admission: Free
Phone: 698-7986
Address: 4888 68th Street SE, Caledonia,
              southeast of Grand Rapids

Maple Sugaring

When the sap begins running from trees in late February or early March, many nature centers demonstrate how maple trees are tapped. Exhibits and slide presentations are often part of the program.

Because many schools schedule field trips to nature centers during this time, you might want to visit late in the day or on weekends to avoid crowds.

Dates/Hours: Check with your local nature center for details (see The "Great Outdoors" for those in the West Michigan area)

Summer

County Fairs

First-rate entertainment lures thousands of fairgoers to county fairs each year. Kids will enjoy the animal shows and competitions, where their peers proudly display the animals they have carefully raised. Midway rides, parades, exhibits, tractor pulls, demolition derbies, horse races, concessions, and wacky contests also play a big part in fair-going excitement.

In western Michigan, fairs take place from July through September. Three of the larger fairs are Allegan County's, Kalamazoo County's, and Ionia's. Call the Michigan Association of Fairs and Exhibitions at 673-3030 for an events calendar, or check with your local Convention and Visitor Bureau or newspaper for details.

Farmers' Markets

The array of fresh fruits, vegetables, and baked breads displayed at a farmer's market is a delight to the senses. Visit just to enjoy the sights and smells, or stock up on seasonal produce.

Benton Harbor

Set up for wholesalers, but with $5 permit, individuals can buy produce. May–October daily and Sunday 8–3. Saturday 8–noon. 1891 Territorial Road east of Crystal and west of Euclid. Phone: 925-0681.

Grand Haven

Early June–late October, Wednesday and Saturday 8–7. July–August, also Monday 1–7. Chinook Pier, Harbor Street.

Grand Rapids

May–September, Tuesday, Wednesday, Friday, Saturday 7:30–4:30. 1147 E. Fulton, just west of Fuller. Phone: 459-8287.

Muskegon

First Saturday in May–Saturday before Christmas. Wednesday, Friday, Saturday 7–5. Center at Baker.

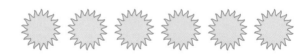

174

U-Pick Fruits and Vegetables

Western Michigan boasts many U-Pick farms. Plan a few hours of berry picking for the freshest, finest foods in Michigan. Call before you go to check availability of the produce, and to find out if your chosen farm has minimum age restrictions. Bring containers, and please leave pets at home.

We advise short trips and play clothes for younger children. Also, keep in mind that blueberries and raspberries are smaller and take longer to pick. Apples and peaches are nice, because kids see full baskets sooner. Our raspberries never make it home!

Order the Farm Market and U-Pick Directories by calling (517) 373-1050, or check the classified ads in your local newspaper.

Dates/Hours: Vary; call farms for information
Admission: Pay for what you pick
Phone: (517) 373-1050

Grand Haven

Annual Sand Sculpture Contest

Test your sculpting skills at Grand Haven's annual sand sculpting competition. You might bring home a trophy or ribbon!

Competitive divisions include families, teams, individuals, and children under 12. Registration is 9–9:45 A.M.

Dates/Hours:	Varies, but always on a June Saturday, 10 A.M.–noon.
Admission:	State park $4 daily, or use your seasonal sticker; park outside free
Phone:	842-4910
Address:	Grand Haven State Park Beach

Grand Haven

Boardwalk and Musical Fountain

Walk 2½ miles along the Grand Haven harbor to the pier. Kids will enjoy walking past marinas and charter fishing boats, window shopping, and perhaps tasting a treat at one of the many restaurants along the way. One of our favorites is the Grand Haven classic, a "Pronto Pup."

Park benches and grassy areas are perfect lookouts for people-watching and boat-watching.

The "world's largest musical fountain" delights thousands of tourists every summer with a half-hour light and music show that you can see from downtown's Waterfront Stadium. After your stroll on the boardwalk, find a spot for your blanket, and enjoy!

The musical fountain pumps 40,000 gallons of water 125 feet into the air to a light classical or popular musical beat. Colored lights add to the show's impressive effects. The show attracts big weekend crowds and plenty of boats.

Dates/Hours:	The boardwalk is very scenic anytime, any season. Musical fountain: Memorial Day–Labor Day evenings at dusk
Admission:	Free, donations for musical fountain accepted
Phone:	1-800-303-4095; 842-4910
Address:	U.S. 31 to Harbor Drive toward Grand Haven State Park. Waterfront Stadium is located at the end of Washington and Main Street near the channel

177

Grand Rapids

Summer in the City

Downtown Grand Rapids has plenty for kids to enjoy on summer Saturdays through September: free horse-and-carriage rides, live entertainment, a fun-and-games arena, karoake, street performers, clown and balloons, a fishing pond, the Funimagination Station, and food booths.

Free concerts are also offered Tuesday, Wednesday, and Friday evenings, featuring blues, country, and oldies.

Dates/Hours: Every Saturday, 12–3 P.M.
Admission: Free
Phone: 459-8287
Address: Monroe Mall, downtown Grand Rapids

Muskegon

Parties in the Park

A great way to get revved up for a summer weekend, Muskegon's Parties in the Park offer relaxed fun, music, food, beverages, and children's events. Most of all, the parties offer folks a chance to get together and gab.

This is a very popular Friday evening event in Muskegon.

Dates/Hours: Fridays, June–August
Admission: Free
Phone: 737-6710
Address: Hackley Park, Muskegon

Pentwater

Summer Beckons!

In addition to a hot sandy beach at Mears State Park, Pentwater has retained its small-town atmosphere, from Thursday evening concerts on the green to August's Homecoming Parade. It also offers a variety of family sports activities, such as swimming, windsurfing, bicycling, beaching, pier fishing, and charter fishing. Tennis is available at public courts, or by membership at Pentwater Tennis Club.

Pentwater has two other great features: an enormous play structure at the Pentwater school and the Dari Creme at the corner of the Beach Road and Main Street. Our kids spent many nickles and dimes at Birdland, an old-fashioned general store.

Bring your smiles — you'll meet folks from all over the region. Regular summer visitors have forged lifelong friendships in Pentwater.

Phone: Chamber of Commerce, 869-4150

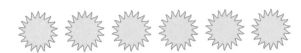

South Haven

Sherman's Dairy Bar

Located right next to its own ice cream plant, Sherman's produces a variety of top-quality ice creams. Stop by for a cone after a long, hard day at the beach!

Dates/Hours: Summer 11–11. Winter 3–9
Admission: Price of your goodies
Phone: 637-8251
Address: I-196 at Phoenix exit, west of South Haven

SEASONAL FUN

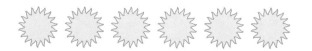

Fall

Apple Cider Mills and Orchards:
A Delicious Expedition

Western Michigan's climate is perfect for fruit growing. Orchards draw crowds all summer for cherry, peach, and blueberry crops, and in autumn, apples. Michigan is the nation's third largest apple producer, with 900,000 trees in Kent County alone!

Enjoy a fall day in rural Michigan — take a bushel basket, and pick from any of the hundreds of varieties of apples at one of the following orchards, from those listed in the local classified ads, or from the U-Pick Directory (order by calling (517) 373-1050). Cider mills are in full swing, too!

Allegan

Dendel Orchards
2860 127th Avenue
673-4317
Cider mill, U-pick apples, farm market.

Augusta

Hillcrest Orchards
7289 N. 46th Street
731-4312
Cider mill, U-pick apples, pumpkins, baked goods, market, picnic area. Fall tours.

SEASONAL FUN

Caledonia

Hilton Apple Acres
2893 108th Street, Caledonia
891-8019
Peaches, apples, plums, pears, and more to pick. Bakery, cider mill, craft shop, picnic area, and farm animals to pet. Hayrides, pumpkin patch, and orchard tours by appointment. $4\frac{1}{4}$ miles west of M-37 on 108th Street. Or U.S. 131 to Caledonia, 100th Street exit. East two miles to Kalamazoo Avenue, south 1 mile to 108th Street, then east $\frac{3}{4}$ mile. Open July 1–December 24. Monday–Saturday 9–6, Tuesday 9–8.

Climax

Canaan Farm Orchard
14810 Roof Drive
746-4066
Cider mill, pumpkins, U-pick apples, market, picnic area. Tours in season.

Dowagiac

Sprague's Old Orchard
33085 Middle Crossing Road
782-2058
Cider mill, U-pick apples, market, pumpkins.

Fennville

Crane's Cider Mill
6054 124th Avenue
561-2297
Cider mill, U-pick apples, pumpkins.

Grand Rapids

Robinette's Apple Haus and Barn Shops
3142 4 Mile Road NE, Grand Rapids. 4 miles
north of I-96 on East Beltline
361-5567
*Open year-round, Monday–Saturday 9–6, Sunday
1–6. Cider mill, bakery (with lunches), gift shop with
large Christmas section. Hayrides. Tours available in
September and October. Winter cross-country skiing,
rentals available.*

Sandy Hill Farm
4905 Peach Ridge NW, Grand Rapids
784-3043
*Apples and strawberries. Visit May – October. Bring a
picnic and enjoy the scenic hilltop view.*

Sietsema Orchards & Cider Mill
3271 Knapp NE, Grand Rapids
363-5921 or 363-0698
*I-96 to East Beltline, two miles north on East Beltline
to Knapp, east on Knapp, 300 feet. Open July–May,
Monday–Saturday 8–6. Wide variety of fruits, cider,
honey, popcorn, and much more. Fall tours.*

Hastings

Cotant's Farm Market
2712 Bedford Road
945-4180
*Cider mill, pumpkins, baked goods, market. Fall
tours.*

185

Kalamazoo

Verhage Fruit Farms
8619 W. ML Avenue
375-0153
*Cider mill, pumpkins, baked goods, U-pick apples,
picnic area. Tours first half of October. Call ahead.*

Lowell

Orchard Hill Apple and Angus Farm
9896 Cascade Road, Lowell. Open August
1–January 1 daily 9–6.
868-7229
*U-pick apples, pears, cherries, pumpkins, vegetables;
bakery, cider mill, farm animals, demonstration
beehive, maple syrup display, and tours. Wagon rides
by appointment.*

Middleville

Historic Bowens Mills
11691 Old Bowens Mills Road
795-7530
*Cider mill, pumpkins, baked goods, market, picnic
area. Wagon rides by appointment.*

Moline

Ritz's Farm Market
910 144th Street
877-4732
*Open July-February. Cider mill, pumpkins, baked
goods, market. Wagon rides by appointment. Tours.*

Rockford

Grass Lake Farm Market
6182 Belding Road, Rockford. Across from Lake
Bella Vista between Rockford and Belding. Open
May–November, Tuesday–Saturday 9-6, Sunday in
September–October 12-5.
874-7194
*Enormous variety of in-season produce, from
asparagus to cherries, watermelons, apples, and
flowers. Orchard tours and hayrides during harvest.*

Battle Creek

The Great Zoo Boo

"Merry, not scary" is the theme of the Binder Park Zoo's Great Zoo Boo, held in October. Children under 13 can trick-or-treat at the zoo among tons of jack-o-lanterns. Zoo staff wears its Halloween finery, too.

Nearly 60,000 visit during this annual event, an especially fun one for young Halloweeners!

Dates/Hours:	Third week in October through Halloween
Admission:	$2.50
Phone:	979-1351
Address:	7400 Division Drive. Three miles south of I-94 off Exit 100 (Beadle Lake Road)

Fall

SEASONAL FUN

Coloma

Farmer Friday's Spooky Halloween Barn

At Farmer Friday's 20,000-square-foot grocery and Halloween store, grocery clerks dress in costumes and have fic-
tional names like Elvis and Lucy. Kids will love the huge
array of disgusting (we mean really grotesque!) masks and
costumes, presidents' heads, wigs, and fake body parts for
sale or rent.

Open year-round, Farmer Friday's attracts customers
from all over the Midwest. Besides serving regular folks,
the store also supplies costumes for theater groups and
schools. Choose from over 500 masks, ranging from $2.98
to $279; costumes rent for $10–$50.

The children's costume area has gobs of masks and
costumes, and plastic noses for under $1, all displayed to
wonderful effect. There is also a Haunted Fun Barn, with
creepy characters, moving floors, and illusions.

Dates/Hours: Monday–Saturday 9–8, Sunday 9–7
Admission: Free to browse; Fun Barn $2
Phone: 468-5512
Address: I-94 west toward Chicago, exit 39 to
              Coloma

Fall

SEASONAL FUN

189

Cooperssville-Marne

Railway Train Rides

Today's kids are more likely to have traveled by jet than by train — no kidding! Choose one of these trips for a memorable outing:

Great Pumpkin Train: Pick out a pumpkin at the railroad station's enormous pumpkin patch after your one-hour ride. Cider and donuts are served on board.

Santa Train: Features strolling musicians, carol sing-along, storytellers, and a special visit from Santa. $1\frac{1}{4}$ hour ride, with cider and donuts provided.

The Railway also offers weekend rides, and group reservations are taken for April, May, and June.

Dates/Hours: Theme rides on weekends. Saturday:
11:30 A.M., 1:00, 2:30, 4:00 P.M.
Sunday: 1:30 and 3:00 P.M.

Admission: Adults $9; children over 2 $6; under 2 free, and seniors $8

Phone: 949-4778

Address: I-96 west of Grand Rapids, Coopersville exit. Just off the freeway; follow signs

Fall

SEASONAL FUN

190

Ferrysburg

Nightmare on Elm Street

Located on Elm Street in Ferrysburg, the Grand Haven Jaycees' Haunted House features very scary devices and tunnels of horror. oooooooOOOOOOoooo!

Dates/Hours:	Week before Halloween: Thursday 7–11 P.M., Friday 7–12 P.M.
Admission:	$6 per person
Phone:	842-4910
Address:	520 Elm Street, Ferrysburg, just off US 31

Fall

SEASONAL FUN

Grand Rapids

Annual Ghoulfest

Kent Harmonia Orchestra dresses up in Halloween garb and plays its scariest Halloween concert each October. Wear your most creative costumes to vie for prizes in these categories: Ages 0–12, Teen, and Group.

The 1½-hour concert draws 400–500 people, and is a howling good time!

Dates/Hours: Varies from mid-October to Halloween
              Eve, 7:30 P.M.
Admission: Adults $5; 12 and under $3
Phone: 771-3940
Address: Fountain Street Church, 24 Fountain
              Street NE, downtown Grand Rapids

Fall

Grand Rapids

Jaycees Haunted House

Dare to experience this VERY scary haunted house. The Jaycees have gained area-wide recognition for the realistic effects and fright factor of their haunted house.

Older kids will love it; but please don't bring children under age 6.

Dates/Hours:	October, 6 P.M.–12:30 A.M. most days (check newspaper for exact times); 1–10 P.M. Halloween Day
Admission:	$6 per person
Phone:	235-4653
Address:	25 Ottawa SW, just south of Fulton Street, downtown Grand Rapids

Fall

SEASONAL FUN

193

Grand Rapids

Robinette's Haunted Hayride

This popular event takes place after dark, outside, and sometimes under a full moon! It's a spooky ride through apple orchards inhabited by gruesome characters and witches.

Although this one is not recommended for kids under 10, our junior-high kids didn't think it was excessively horrifying. Free cider is handed out by witches who dance around the fire.

Call ahead for reservations if you have a large group.

Dates/Hours:	October
Admission:	$9.50 per person
Phone:	361-5567
Address:	Northwest corner of East Beltline and 4 Mile Road

Grand Rapids

"Screams in the Dark" at Maze Craze

Make your way through a giant labyrinth and eat lots of pizza. Maze Craze offers monthly theme parties, including October's VERY frightening Haunted Maze, March's Caribbean party, and Hearts Galore in February, among others.

Schedule a birthday party for your 7–13 year old, and play laser tag — using laser guns with infrared beams — before and after your group does the maze. The charge for birthday parties is $6.25 per person.

Maze Craze offers laser tag before and after regular hours just for the older folks; local businesspeople have been spotted indulging in this wild game.

Dates/Hours:	Tuesday–Thursday 3–9, Friday 3–10, Saturday 11–10, Sunday 1–5; Closed Monday
Admission:	$5. Add $2 for all-you-can-eat pizza, another $1 for all the pop you can drink
Phone:	957-4242
Address:	2845 Thornhills Avenue, south off 28th Street, just east of I-96 exit

Fall

SEASONAL FUN

195

Greenville

The Haunted Mill

For the month of October, Greenville's teen club becomes a Haunted Mill. In a former life, it was a potato-and-grain storage building.

Impressive special effects will scare the hair off a cat . . . a phantom shakes the building, a mad scientist rises out of the cellar, and the Hunchback of Notre Dame rings bells.

The Haunted Mill is not suitable for children under 7 years old.

Dates/Hours: Every evening in October, 7:30 P.M.
Admission: Adults $10; half price for groups of 13!
Phone: 754-5656, or Greenville Chamber of Commerce 754-5697
Address: U.S. 131 to Greenville exit. 623 N. Lafayette, on Greenville's main street

Fall

SEASONAL FUN

Kent County

"Harvest Trails"

Nearly 30 of Kent County's farms open their doors to the public during fall's first three weekends. Learn about Michigan's agriculture and the diversity of products our state offers.

Each farm is unique, with petting zoos (Shetland sheep, pygmy goats, and miniature horses are among the more unusual), antique tractor displays, pig roasts, and pony rides. Kids will also enjoy musical entertainment, wagon rides, apple and pumpkin picking, scarecrow making, a children's maze, and hands-on art projects.

Contact the Kent County Farm Bureau, MSU Cooperative Extension Service, or any D&W Food Center for brochures and maps of participating farms.

Dates/Hours:	Last weekend in September, first two weekends in October; hours vary
Admission:	Free. Products for sale at some farms
Phone:	451-8065, or MSU Co-op. Ext. Svc. 336-3265
Address:	Various locations; check map

Fall

SEASONAL FUN

197

Winter

Cut Your Own Christmas Tree

Michigan ranks number one nationally in the live Christmas tree industry, harvesting more than 6.5 million trees per year. Call ahead to these West Michigan tree farms to find out if they are U-Cuts, retail, or wholesale operations:

Benton Harbor–St. Joseph

> Yule-Tide Acres
> 8466 M-62, Berrien Center
> 461-3111

Grand Haven–Holland

> Centennial Farms*
> 17594 Hickory Road, Spring Lake
> 847-0348

> DeLass Farm Market
> 813 W. Savidge, Spring Lake
> 842-1122

> E & R Tree Farms*
> 10170 76th Avenue, Allendale
> 895-4932

> Evergreen Farm Nursery*
> 13894 168th, Grand Haven
> 842-2260

Glueck's Evergreen Acres*
15901 Ferris at U.S. 31, Grand Haven
842-9398

Holland Nursery Outlet*
12683 Greenly
399-3851

Luurtsema Tree Farm*
5279 Bauer Road, Hudsonville
669-7885

Michigreen Nursery
12777 N. Cedar Drive
842-3537

Northland Christmas Tree Company
10845 Lake Michigan Drive, W. Olive
846-4170

Pine Ridge Nursery & Wreath
10658 158th, W. Olive
842-8936

Ruch's Tree Farm West*
U.S. 31 just south of M-45, W. Olive
842-4576

Stone's Evergreen
8518 146th Avenue, Olive Township
399-2124

Twin Oaks Christmas Tree Farms
15323 Mercury Drive
846-3766

Van Slooten Tree Farms
10606 168th Avenue, W. Olive
847-6023

Van's Pines*
7550 144th Avenue, Olive Township
399-1620

Greater Grand Rapids

Church's
182 136th Street, Grant
834-7158
Horsedrawn wagon rides on weekends

Duddles
U.S. 131, Exit 159 Ashton, Reed City
832-2731
Tours, field of trees, gift shop

DeWaal Malefyt
6226 Van Buren, Hudsonville
875-8268

Honey Tree Nursery
934 — 129th Avenue, Bradley
792-9317
Horse-drawn sleigh rides at Christmas

Hutsons
878 N. Greenville Road, Greenville
754-7665
Wagon rides on weekends

Krampe Tree Farm
6930 Childsdale, Rockford
866-2147

*Featured in the Tri-Cities' Christmas Tree Festival.

Winter

SEASONAL FUN

Lenderink Family Tree Farm
1271 House Road, Belmont
881-8257

Pierces
4501 Baseline Road, Bellevue
965-7403

Pinecroft
5313 Bauer Road, Hudsonville
669-6351

Thornapple Valley Pines
1700 McCann Road, Middleville
772-6157

Greater Kalamazoo

Almena Tree Farms
23734 County Road 375, Mattawan
668-3212

Motts Christmas Barn
16540 S. 21st, Schoolcraft
649-3866

U-Cut Christmas Trees
Wahmhoff's, 23090 M-40, Gobles
628-4308

Muskegon

Slocum Brothers Tree Farm
RFD 3, Hart
873-3706

Toys for Tots —
Kids Who Give Also Receive

Children learn about the true spirit of Christmas in giving toys to children who otherwise might find nothing under the tree. Toys for Tots works in western Michigan, thanks to hard-working U.S. Marines, donor organizations, and hundreds of volunteers.

Just before Thanksgiving, barrels for toy donations are placed in many western Michigan business and retail locations.

In the Grand Rapids area, the annual campaign is kicked off in late November with an evening children's party at the Amway Grand Plaza's Ambassador Ballroom. Admission for your child is one unwrapped toy. He or she may visit with Santa and have fun and refreshments.

Dates/Hours: Thanksgiving–one week before Christmas
Phone: 363-1699
Address: Donation barrels located throughout
            western Michigan (and the U.S.)

Grand Haven

Giant Nativity Scene

Bundle up warmly for the story of Christ's birth on Dewey Hill at the Waterfront Stadium. Lights illuminate the players during the 12-minute show. Strains of carols drift across the water as a golden star joins the others in the night sky.

Enjoy the sight of 44-foot wooden figures "coming to life" as they tell the story of the first Christmas.

Dates/Hours: December 1–24, 7–9 P.M.
Admission: Free
Phone: 842-2550 or 842-4499
Address: Waterfront Stadium. Take I-96 west to Grand Haven exit

Hastings

"Of Christmas Past"

Charlton Park Village, Museum and Recreation Area is located on Thornapple River and Lake Charlton, just east of Hastings. In the 17-building village, park staff and volunteers lovingly recapture late 19th-century Christmases with activities for people of all ages.

Dressed in Victorian costumes, the group plays live music, makes old-fashioned ornaments, bakes cookies, roasts chestnuts, and provides hands-on activities and craft demonstrations. Children will enjoy visiting St. Nicholas and shopping for stocking stuffers in the museum. Be sure to save time for a sleigh ride!

The museum also offers a variety of field trips, tours, and educational programs. Students may even spend a day as children of the 1890s.

Dates/Hours:	First and second weekends in December, Saturday–Sunday 12–5
Admission:	$4 adults; ages 5-15 $1; under 5 free
Phone:	945-3775
Address:	M-37 to M-79 south of Hastings, turn east, 4 miles north on Charlton Park Road

Winter

SEASONAL FUN

Holland

Annual Celebration of St. Nicholas

Some say Dutch Village is Holland's most delightful attraction — at Christmas time, this is no doubt true! The ten-acre theme park is splendid, with over 10,000 lights, garlands, and a life-sized nativity scene in the barn. Sinterklaas (St. Nicholas) even pays visits!

At Dutch Village, the Holland Community Players present *Sinterklaas Comes to Molendorp,* an original play that has delighted thousands. Caroling follows if weather permits.

Plan to treat the children to Dutch cuisine at the on-premises Queen's Inn Restaurant, and visit the area's best import shops for extra-special Christmas gifts.

Dates/Hours:	Theater: Thanksgiving to the week before Christmas, matinees and evening performances
Admission:	Theater: $6–$14.95 (with or without lunch/dinner). Dutch Village: regular admission (adults $5; children $3)
Phone:	1-800-822-2770 or 396-4221
Address:	U.S. 31, in front of Outlets of Holland

Kalamazoo

Festival of Trees

Begin the Christmas holiday season by viewing Kalamazoo's annual display of Christmas trees, each sponsored by an area business and beautifully decorated.

The trees, a children's crafts area, gingerbread village, gift shop, family songfest, and family night holiday brunch all appeal to children. Santa also takes time from his busy schedule to visit.

Sponsored by Junior League of Kalamazoo.

Dates/Hours:	Third weekend in November, Thursday–Saturday 10–9, Sunday 1–5
Admission:	Varies according to activity
Phone:	342-5562
Address:	Wings Stadium Annex: I-94 to Sprinkle Road exit, south just off the freeway

Winter

SEASONAL FUN

Plainwell

Echo Valley Toboggan Parties

Tobogganing is fun and fast, and makes a great winter activity for kids and families. Visit one of western Michigan's most famous toboggan parks, Echo Valley, with its eight lighted chutes, each ¼ mile long. Toboggans are included with admission. All runs are well supervised for safety.

Echo Valley also maintains a huge outdoor skating rink with music and lights; skate rentals are available. The warming lodge has a fireplace and concessions.

Sledders, also check out Greater Grand Rapids hills listed in "Active Sports."

Dates/Hours: Winter, weather permitting:
                   Friday 7–11 P.M., Saturday 1–11 P.M.,
                   Sunday 1–11. Closed Christmas
Admission: Adults $7; 12 and under $6
Phone: 349-3291
Address: U.S. 131 to Plainwell exit, 20 miles north
                   of Kalamazoo. East to H Avenue, then to
                   8495 W. H Avenue

Saugatuck

A Christmas Carol

Chase away the holiday blues with Scrooge and Tiny Tim during this annual performance set in a beautiful Gothic church.

Stay for the Christmas Parade, ride a horse-and-carriage through town, tour the area's historic homes, and browse the shops.

Dates/Hours:	Second and third weekends in December
Admission:	$7 per ticket, after October
Phone:	857-1701
Address:	First Congregational Church, Saugatuck

Winter

SEASONAL FUN

Spring Lake

Annual Polar Ice Cap Golf Tournament

Brrrrrr! Imagine playing golf on the last Saturday in January. Then do it!

This special tournament, sponsored by the Grand Haven Jaycees, has children's, adults', and team divisions. Play is conducted by U.S.G.A. Winter Rules, and you may golf 9 or 18 holes. Children's activities are available too.

Dates/Hours:	Last Saturday in January, 9–3
Admission:	18 holes: foursome $24, one person $7.
	9 holes: foursome $16, one person $5.
	Under 12 $2
Phone:	842-4910
Address:	Spring Lake Country Club, 17496 N. Fruitport Road, Spring Lake

FESTIVALS

Tips for Happy Families
at Festivals and Parades*

- Wear play clothes, especially for hands-on activities and food!
- Wear comfortable shoes for tired feet.
- Bring water to drink.
- Bring small snacks (cereal or crackers).
- Bring a blanket for resting.
- Leave pets at home.
- Wear sunscreen and sun hats.
- Use kiddie leashes in crowds.
- Festival programs are well publicized — take advantage of youth shows and kids' activities. Pick short events for young children.

Two kinds of festivals that are too numerous to list in this section are the many ethnic celebrations and the parades and fireworks that take place every year in western Michigan.

You can enlarge your child's world by exposing him or her to the traditions and cultures of other peoples. What better way to learn about Native Americans, Hispanics, African Americans, and Europeans is there than to celebrate their heritages at special events and festivals? Check out the art, crafts, legends, traditions, music, dances, and sports. Our kids thoroughly enjoy the excursions, and we hope to continue visiting a few new ethnic festivals each year.

*Provided by Grand Rapids' Festival organizers

Parades are usually centered around holidays like the Fourth of July, and make wonderful excursions for children, especially when communities show off their distinct local personalities.

We recommend that you check with your area Convention and Visitor Bureau or Chamber of Commerce for information about ethnic festivals and parade schedules and routes (see pages 385-88).

West Michigan Festival Calendar

January

> Snow'Fly
> Kalamazoo
> 383-8778

> Annual Polar Ice Golf Tournament
> Grand Haven/Spring Lake
> 842-4910

> Winterfest
> Gun Lake
> 672-7822

> Winterfest
> Coloma-Watervliet
> 463-8166

Late January–February

> Winterfest
> Grand Haven
> 842-4910, 463-8166

April

> Children's Street Fair
> Grand Rapids
> 456-3361

> Spring Arts Festival
> Franciscan Farm & Life Process Center–Lowell
> 897-7842

May

Trillium Festival
Muskegon–Gillette Nature
Center–P. J. Hoffmaster Park
798-3573

Kitefest
Kalamazoo
383-8776

Tulip Time
Holland
1-800-822-2770

Very Special Arts Festival
Kent County classrooms
451-0937

June

Festival of the Arts
Grand Rapids
1-800-678-9859

Cereal Festival
Battle Creek
962-2240

Kalamazoo Air Show
Kalamazoo
381-8237

July

Muskegon Summer Celebration
Muskegon
722-3751

216

International Cherry Pit Spitting Championships
Eau Claire
782-7107

Hot Air Balloon Championship
Battle Creek
962-0592

Kindleberger Festival of Performing Arts
349-3785

Muskegon Air Fair
Muskegon County Airport
798-4596

Taste of Kalamazoo
Downtown Kalamazoo
385-6200

Flowerfest
Kalamazoo
381-3597

August

Black Arts Festival
Kalamazoo
349-1035

Coast Guard Festival
Grand Haven
842-4910

Fiberfest
Kalamazoo
765-3047

217

Abbott's Magic Get-Together
Colon
432-3235

Blueberry Festival
South Haven
637-5171

Labor Day Weekend

Muskegon Shoreline Spectacular
Pere Marquette Park
737-5791

September

Celebration on the Grand
Grand Rapids
456-2675

Festival of the Arts
Kalamazoo
342-5059

West Michigan Children's Festival
John Ball Zoo/Grand Rapids
456-3361

Late September-October

Fall Fest
Fallasburg Park
897-9161

October

Ocktoberfest/Rocktoberfest
Kalamazoo
385-6200

Red Flannel Festival
Cedar Springs
696-2262

Harvest Festival
Rockford
866-2000

November–December

Festival of Lights
Battle Creek–Binder Park Zoo
979-1351

Michigan Christmas Tree Festival
Grand Haven, Holland, Zeeland
396-4221

December 31

Midnight at the Creek
Battle Creek
964-3700

New Year's Fest
Kalamazoo
381-4003

Spring

Grand Rapids

Children's Street Fair

At this grand 16-year-old event, children are IT! Stage entertainment, children's singers, clowns, tumblers, a petting zoo, and play area are all part of the fun. Cookie Monster and Captain Kangaroo have appeared in past years!

Child-related organizations have booths with FREE fun or educational activities — it may be bubbles, shaving cream, or who knows what?

Geared toward 2–8 year olds, The Children's Street Fair is a biggie in the kid-pleasing arena. This event is coordinated by the Michigan Association for the Education of Young Children and sponsored by several area businesses.

Dates/Hours:	Last Saturday in April, 10–2
Admission:	Free
Phone:	456-3361
Address:	Calder Plaza, downtown Grand Rapids

221

Grand Rapids

Spring Splash Children's Carnival

A festive one-day event for kids and their families, with games, prizes, clowns, spacewalk, storytelling, concessions, and more!

This is a relatively small event with a school carnival atmosphere. It IS held at a school, and most kids LOVE school carnivals!

Dates/Hours: Mid-April Saturday, 10:30–6
Admission: Free admission, $.25 per event ticket
Phone: 949-5300
Address: Grand Rapids Baptist College, west side of East Beltline, north of I-96

Grand Rapids

Very Special Arts Festival

The Very Special Arts Festival held each May aims to provide educational opportunities in the arts for special-needs students. These kids participate in dance, drawing, music, and visual workshops — 97 in all — given by professional artists.

Most of the activities take place in Kent County classrooms, where at least a third of the students have special needs.

Although this festival is not open to the general public, you may obtain permission to attend. Call 451-0937 for information. Funding and organization is provided by the Junior League, which needs volunteers to help with programs.

Spring

Phone: 451-0937

Tulip Time Festival

Celebrate the Dutch heritage with millions of blooming tulips, parades, fireworks, musical shows, street scrubbing, and more than 1400 *klompen* dancers.

- **Volksparade:** A brigade of costumed street scrubbers cleans the street until it shines. Then on with a two-hour parade.
- **Children's Costume Parade:** Hundreds of schoolchildren in costume enthusiastically show off banners and signs.
- **Parade of Bands:** The grand finale begins with *klompen* dancers, over 50 premier bands, and floats along a two-mile route.

Over 500,000 people visit Holland during Tulip Time, the U.S.'s fifth largest festival!

Dates/Hours:	Ten days in early May. Full schedule each day, beginning at 8:30 A.M.
Admission:	Charges vary significantly by event Parades are free, except for $3–$4 bleacher seats
Phone:	1-800-822-2770 for schedules.
Address:	Events are held throughout Holland

Kalamazoo

Kitefest

Five thousand to 7,500 participants join in as Kitefest celebrates summer, with kites everywhere! Kitefest offers two days of just-for-fun competitions, contests, games, and prizes.

First-time visitors will be amazed to find that kites have gone high-tech — from popular triangular kites made with plastic sails to multi-line kites maneuvered in aerobic stunts.

Kalamazoo County Recreation Department has hosted Kitefest for over ten years, and puts on a dozen other fun and competitive events at county parks from mid-May to mid-September. Call 383-8778 for information.

Dates/Hours: Mid-May weekend, Saturday–Sunday 9–5
Admission: $3 per carload
Phone: 383-8778
Address: River Oaks Park. Kalamazoo I-94 east to exit 85. North 1 mile on M-96; watch for signs

225

Muskegon

Trillium Festival

Pay tribute to Michigan's wildflowers! Guided wildflower hikes, children's activities (kids get to make trillium pinwheels), photo exhibit, and slide shows are all part of this festival. Kids especially enjoy trolley rides — call for departure times. Bring binoculars for the 8 A.M. bird hike.

Adults will also appreciate plant and book sales, gardening lectures, and the art show.

Dates/Hours: Mother's Day weekend, Saturday–Sunday
              10–5. Also open Tuesday–Friday 1–5
Admission: Free to public with state park permit
Phone: 798-3573
Address: Gillette Nature Center, P. J. Hoffmaster
              State Park, Muskegon

Summer

Battle Creek

International Hot Air Balloon Championship

Over one million spectators are on hand for the display of up to 150 hot air balloons ascending into the sky. What a sight!

Balloons are launched from 6:30 A.M. to 6 P.M., weather permitting. Other activities include an amusement park with 35 rides, fireworks on July 2 and 4, and a full-fledged air show. The concert entertainment draws top performers.

This event will soon be moving from "International Championship" status to "World Championship," meaning it will become even larger in future years.

Dates/Hours: Fourth of July week
Admission: July 2–4: $4 daily. July 5–9: $2 daily.
              Parking $4 daily per vehicle, $10 for
              RVs. Children under 3 feet tall free
Phone: 962-0592
Address: Kellogg Airport, Battle Creek

227

Battle Creek

World's Longest Breakfast Table and Cereal Festival

Home of Kellogg Cereal, Battle Creek hosts a three-day Cereal Festival every June. A highlight is "The World's Longest Breakfast Table," where 40,000 people are served at least 40,000 bowls of cereal. The table stretches to the city limits.

The Jaycees sponsor a Cereal Festival raft race. Build your racing raft, and join the crowd. A running race and walk are also featured.

Dates/Hours: Second weekend in June. Breakfast hours
               are 8:30 A.M.–1 P.M.
Admission: Free
Phone: 963-0670 or 962-2240
Address: Michigan Avenue, downtown Battle Creek

Colon

Abbott's Magic Get-Together

Colon is the magic capital of the world. For four days in mid-August, magic lovers from around the world congregate in this small community for the almost 60-year-old Magic Festival. Everyone is invited!

Professional magicians perform in evening magic shows for the public. There is also a stage contest for kids who perform feats of magic.

Colon is also home of the world's largest mail-order magic supply company, Abbott's Magic Manufacturing. Showroom salespeople demonstrate magic tricks. Open Monday–Friday 8–5, Saturday 8–4. Call 432-3235 for information. 124 St. Joseph, Colon.

Dates/Hours:	Four days during second week in August
Admission:	Free
Phone:	For festival information: Abbott's Magic Manufacturing 432-3235
Address:	Colon: Southeast of Kalamazoo, between Three Rivers and Coldwater

Eau Claire

International Cherry Pit Spitting Championship

Held in the rural town of Eau Claire, the Cherry Pit Spitting Championship is just that! Can you imagine how much your children would love to spit their pits against the best pit spitters in the world? Two hundred people compete in the qualifying rounds in Youth, Ladies, Men, and Dignitaries divisions.

This annual event has spanned over 20 years, and attracts 1,000 spectators each year. Other activities include moonlight hayrides, tours, and a cookout.

The contest is held at the beginning of the week-long Eau Claire Area Cherry Festival, which includes a carnival, talent show, and kiddie's fun fair. The finale is a street dance and fireworks. There's also 3-on-3 basketball, 2-person volleyball, a 5k and 10k walk/run, and plenty more.

Dates/Hours:	First Saturday in July
Admission:	Free
Phone:	782-7101
Address:	Tree-Mendus Fruit Farm, 9351 East Eureka Road. I-94, exit 29 just 8 miles east of Dowagiac

Grand Haven

Coast Guard Festival

The official U.S. Coast Guard observance is complete with carnival, entertainment, food, parades, arts-and-crafts shows, a beauty pageant, a 10k, 5k, and 1-mile run, and fireworks.

The Coast Guard Parade is one of the festival's highlights. Fireworks follow the Musical Fountain performance at dusk on the last day of the festival. They can be seen from the Waterfront Stadium, along the boardwalk, and from downtown Grand Haven.

Dates/Hours: Last weekend in July, first week of August
Admission: Free
Phone: 846-5940, Coast Guard office
Address: Downtown Grand Haven

Grand Rapids

Festival of the Arts

The nation's largest all-volunteer arts festival welcomes summer each June with three days of music, dance, and theater performances. Visual-arts displays highlight artists' photography, film, video, painting, and sculpture. Kids will especially enjoy the hands-on art activities and games, and watching young performers.

The variety of ethnic foods offered by over 30 organizations is truly astonishing (and fattening). Plan to sample various treats at Festival!

Dates/Hours: First weekend in June
Admission: Free, although you should plan to eat some of the many ethnic foods (proceeds from food sales benefit sponsoring organizations)
Phone: 459-2787 or 1-800-678-9859
Address: Calder Plaza and surrounding streets, downtown Grand Rapids

Kalamazoo

Black Arts Festival

A family- and kids-oriented event, the Black Arts Festival is preceded by the Children's Day Festival (first Thursday in August), which features youth entertainers, face painting, community organizations' activities, and food.

The Black Arts Festival presents street theater, music, ethnic storytelling, black film, poetry readings, and other fun activities and events. Held at Martin Luther King, Jr. Park in downtown Kalamazoo, it is sponsored by the Black Arts and Cultural Center.

The center has an active class schedule, with art, dance, music, and acting classes offered year-round. A summer theater camp is also held in June.

Dates/Hours: First weekend in August. Call for information about the festival or classes
Admission: Festival: free. Classes: fees vary
Phone: 349-1035
Address: 225 Parsons, Kalamazoo

233

Kalamazoo

Fiberfest, The Festival

This odd-sounding festival is outrageously successful! The largest of its kind in the U.S. and Canada, the two-day festival showcases natural fiber products and animals, and offers a wealth of information for adults and children. Following are some of Fiberfest's kid pleasers:

- **Fiber-Producing Animals:** 700 llamas, Angora rabbits, and goats.
- **Competitions:** Classic Sheep Show, Llama and Alpaca Show, goat-calling contest.
- **Free Kid's Workshops:** felting, weaving, spinning.
- **Demonstrations:** sheep and goat shearing, dog herding, llama handling, yak demonstrations, and more.

Additional attractions include sales and auctions of all types and a llama pet-o-rama.

Dates/Hours:	First weekend in August
Admission:	$5 parking fee; otherwise free
Phone:	765-3047 (Freeport)
Address:	Kalamazoo County Fairgrounds, I-94 to Sprinkle Road exit to Lake Street

Kalamazoo

High on Kalamazoo Air Show

The top-notch performances at the High on Kalamazoo Air Show draw many thousands of spectators annually. Features include aerobatic shows, parachute teams, special planes (Robosaurus), sailplanes, and air-attack reenactments (D-Day). Vintage war planes fly, as do modern civilian/military aircraft. Some are also grounded for viewing.

Children's learning activities take place in the kids' space. The family viewing area is alcohol-free, smoke-free, and fenced for kids' safety.

Air shows are very noisy — bring earplugs for all. Hats, sunscreen, and layered clothing are also musts. You don't want to be deaf and broiled when the show is finished. Bring food in plastic containers — no littering! A large parking area is available south of Milham Road.

Dates/Hours:	Second weekend in June, Friday evening–Sunday
Admission:	Advance tickets, adults $8; children $2 At the gate, adults $5–$10; children $3–$4
Phone:	1-800-945-KALA, or 381-8237
Address:	Kalamazoo/Battle Creek International Airport, Portage Road south off I-94

Kalamazoo

Kindleberger Summer Festival of the Performing Arts

Held at scenic Kindleberger Park, the Summer Festival of the Performing Arts features talented artists from all the disciplines.

The festival includes a musical theater production, children's play, dance recital, arts-and-crafts fair, and Kalamazoo Symphony Orchestra concert. Plan to enter the 5k run or walk, and to watch the festival parade.

Kindleberger Park has 40 acres of rolling, wooded beauty.

Dates/Hours:	Always during the week after July 4th
Admission:	Free
Phone:	349-3785
Address:	I-94, Business loop to Kalamazoo Avenue, turn right, follow to Riverview, then to Park Drive

Kalamazoo

Taste of Kalamazoo

Come with an empty stomach to this delectable three-day festival of food, drink, music, and fun. Food is prepared by chefs from approximately 25 area restaurants.

It's best to take the children during daytime hours — when they're happiest (and hungriest)! Children's Theatre performances and face painting take place Saturday afternoon.

Average cost of each food item is $3, although prices vary from $.50 to $4.

Dates/Hours: Mid-July weekend, 11 A.M.–2 A.M.
Admission: Free during day; 5–7 P.M. $1;
              after 7 P.M. $3
Phone: 385-6200
Address: Water Street Festival Site: Water and
              Kalamazoo Streets, downtown Kalamazoo

237

Muskegon Air Fair

Kids will be enthralled with military, warbird, and civilian flight demonstrations during the three-day Muskegon Air Fair. Bombing missions — the bombing of Pearl Harbor, for example — are reenacted, and over 100 other aircrafts are displayed.

Reserve a table with umbrella at the Flight Club for $99.

The Muskegon Air Fair has grown in popularity each year since it began in 1983. Attendance has grown to 100,000 people in recent years.

Bring earplugs and sunscreen, especially for children.

Dates/Hours: Mid-July weekend 10–6
Admission: Adults $9; children 5–12 $4; 4 and under free; discounts available
Phone: 737-6696 (Air Fair hotline) or 798-4596 ext. 29
Address: Muskegon County Airport, off U.S. 31

Muskegon

Shoreline Spectacular

Help close the summer season with this five-day extrava-
ganza, held over Labor Day weekend. The water-ski show,
children's activities, canine frisbee contest, elephant rides,
carnival, concerts, and sporting events are all guaranteed
to bring smiles!

Dates/Hours:	Labor Day weekend
Admission:	Many free festivals; some entertainment tents have admission fees
Phone:	737-5791
Address:	Pere Marquette Park, along Lake Michigan

Muskegon

Summer Celebration

The week-long Summer Celebration includes a huge parade, fireworks, children's events, carnival and midway rides, and many entertainment tents with nationally renowned performers. The kids might also enjoy village craft demonstrations and food.

Held in Muskegon for over 25 years, the Summer Celebration was formerly called the Great Lumbertown Music Festival.

Dates/Hours: One week in late June/early July
Admission: Buy one button for admission to all entertainment; adults $10, kids $2
Phone: 722-3751 or 722-6520
Address: U.S. 131 to Western Avenue exit, to Heritage Landing

240

South Haven

Blueberry Festival

The world's leading blueberry producer, South Haven, celebrates the harvest with a four-day Blueberry Festival, including parades, a carnival, a dance, a pie-eating contest, arts and crafts, volleyball and basketball tournaments, and sand sculpture.

Also, don't miss the pig roast, fish boil, and more food!

Dates/Hours: Mid-August weekend
Admission: Free
Phone: 637-5171 or 637-5252
Address: Downtown South Haven

Fall

Cedar Springs

Red Flannel Festival

The Red Flannel Festival is a celebration of Cedar Springs' heritage as the Red Flannel Capital of the World, dating back to the lumberjack era.

Held the first weekend in October, the Red Flannel Festival draws 24,000 visitors for the huge arts-and-crafts fair, carnival rides, and downtown flea market. A full run of free fun takes place in an entertainment tent, and other entertainers mingle with the crowds. The highlight, though, is the Red Flannel Parade.

Enjoy a lumberjack-style dinner, too, with stick-to-your-ribs biscuits and gravy.

Dates/Hours:	First weekend in October, Friday evening and Saturday
Admission:	Free
Phone:	696-3260 (call Tuesday–Thursday)
Address:	U.S. 131 to Cedar Springs exit (17 Mile Road); 20 minutes north of Grand Rapids.

Grand Rapids

Celebration on the Grand

This annual community celebration is centered around the Grand River and downtown Grand Rapids, and features continuous entertainment all weekend long.

The Celebration Parade takes place on Thursday. Friday's fireworks are preceded by several band performances, beginning at 5 P.M., and ending in time for spectacular 9:30 fireworks at Ah-Nab-Awen Bicentennial Park.

The Hispanic Festival is celebrated on Calder Plaza the same weekend, and the Indian Lodge Pow Wow takes place at Riverside Park. Sunday is Community Enrichment Day — no admission is charged at the museums, zoo, library, and Belknap Arena.

Dates/Hours: Thursday–Sunday after Labor Day
Admission: Free
Phone: 456-2675
Address: Downtown Grand Rapids, Ah-Nab-Awen Bicentennial Park

Grand Rapids

West Michigan Children's Festival

Fire trucks, police cars, finger printing for kids, craft-projects, booths, and stage entertainers add up to wonderful entertainment for area children in September. Free food — cookies, candy, and juice boxes — is donated by local businesses.

Dates/Hours:	Mid-September Saturday
Admission:	Free
Phone:	456-3361
Address:	John Ball Park: Fulton Street NW

Kalamazoo

Festival of the Arts

For one mid-September weekend, downtown Kalamazoo is transformed into a forum for art. If it has anything to do with the visual and performing arts, it'll be there!

Activities include ceramics, painting, film, music, theater, and dance. Kids will especially enjoy the hands-on Kids' Art Yard. Food is part of the fun, too.

Dates/Hours:	Mid-September weekend: Friday noon–10, Saturday 10–10
Admission:	Free
Phone:	342-5059
Address:	Downtown Kalamazoo Mall

Kalamazoo

NSRA Street Rod National North

Kalamazoo's Street Rod National is an outstanding show and competition for pre-1948 autos, both built from scratch and restored. The cars (some worth many thousands of dollars) and their owners come from all over the country, including Alaska.

Over 3,000 autos and street rods, manufacturer exhibits, arts and crafts, a vintage parts swap meet, live entertainment, a Chevy S-10 giveaway, and games add up to total family fun!

Thousands converge upon the Kalamazoo County Fairgrounds for this event, and Kalamazoo's hotels are booked solid by March. Plan ahead to visit one of Kalamazoo's biggest events!

Dates/Hours:	Mid-September weekend, Friday–Saturday 9–6, Sunday 9–2
Admission:	Adults $10; kids 6–12 $3; under 6 free
Phone:	(303) 776-7841 (Colorado)
Address:	Kalamazoo County Fairgrounds, Kalamazoo

Winter

Battle Creek

Midnight at the Creek

Battle Creek's family New Year's Eve celebration is held at 12 downtown locations, with nonalcoholic entertainment that includes storytellers, music of all kinds, ice-skating, tasty treats, and fireworks to ring in the New Year.

This is a big family event. Buy one button per person and get into all events. A shuttle bus provides transportation to each location.

Dates/Hours: December 31, 6 P.M.–midnight
Admission: Buy a Midnight at the Creek button for each person
Phone: 764-3700
Address: Downtown Battle Creek

Battle Creek

Zoolights Festival

Visit Battle Creek's Binder Park Zoo where over 170,000 sparkling lights set the festive mood for Zoolights. Live animals, lighted animal displays, crafts, and entertainment are featured.

This special event was formerly called Christmas at the Zoo.

Dates/Hours: Third weekend in November–December 30 (except December 24–25)

Admission: $2.50; under 6 free (or by height)

Phone: 979-1351

Address: 7400 Division Drive. Three miles south of I-94, exit 100 (Beadle Lake Road)

Coloma/Watervliet

Winterfest

Celebrate winter with a combination of indoor activities and outdoor sports. Sponsored by Coloma-Watervliet businesses, Winterfest promotes snowmobile races, euchre, cribbage, a softball tournament, entertainment, and food.

The Annual Ice Sculpturing Competition is held on Watervliet's Main Street on Saturday and Sunday during Winterfest. Two hundred-pound ice blocks are sculpted by chefs from Notre Dame, who create 60 works of art! Call 463-6635 for information about the competition.

Dates/Hours: Last weekend in January
Admission: Free
Phone: 463-8166
Address: Coloma-Watervliet parks, Paw Paw Lake, and area businesses

251

Grand Haven, Spring Lake, Ferrysburg

Winterfest

Winterfest is a ten-day celebration of winter's indoor AND outdoor activities. The calendar is loaded with community events, with highlights taking place on the weekends. Kids can snow ski, ice-skate, and watch dogsled races at Mulligan's Hollow Park.

At Children's Creation (First and Columbus Streets), kids can make crafts, listen to stories, and watch a gerbil race! Food is available, too.

Winterfest also features art exhibits, racquetball tournaments, outdoor volleyball, a chili cook-off, a pool tournament, euchre tournaments, and ski/snowboard races.

Dates/Hours:	Last week of January through the first week of February
Admission:	Free
Phone:	842-4910
Address:	Downtown Grand Haven

Kalamazoo

New Year's Fest

Kalamazoo hosts a nonalcoholic family celebration of performing arts every New Year's Eve. Many groups of musical entertainers, jugglers, dancers, and magicians perform continuously in downtown churches and civic buildings. The Yo-Yo Man and storytellers are very popular with the kids.

More than 7,000 visitors help to ring in the New Year with spectacular fireworks. The holiday decorations are outstanding in downtown's Bronson Park — kids especially seem to like walking under the candy cane arches.

Dates/Hours: December 31, 5:30 P.M.–midnight
Admission: Adults $10; children $7
Phone: 387-4185
Address: Downtown Kalamazoo

Lakeshore Area

Michigan Christmas Tree Festival

Celebrate the holiday season with a visit to Christmas tree plantations, Dutch Village, unique shops, arts-and-crafts shows, and the Classic Homes Tour.

Michigan is the nation's leader in plantation tree production, harvesting over 6.5 million trees per year. Visit the farms taking part in the Christmas Tree Festival — those in Grand Haven, Holland, and Zeeland are on our list in "Seasonal Fun" — for great times, and great bargains.

Call 842-4499 for a map and complete listing of festival events.

Dates/Hours:	Thanksgiving to Christmas Eve
Admission:	See listing and call ahead
Phone:	842-4499
Address:	Consult map

AMUSEMENT PLUS

Family Amusement Centers

Some family amusement centers are described on other pages in this section. Please be sure that your children, for their safety, are supervised at all times. These places feature driving ranges, batting cages, mini-golf, basketball, arcades, go-carts, bumper boats, kiddie boats and rides, and ball crawls; call specific centers for more information.

Battle Creek

Bally's Aladdin's Castle
5775 Beckley Road
979-4747

Hit-Em Here
1790 E. Columbia
965-5221

Riverview Recreation
2000 E. Columbia
963-5838

Benton Harbor–St. Joseph

Action Territory Family Fun
1550 Mall Drive
925-5000

Captain Mike's Fun Park
10975 S. Red Arrow Highway, Bridgman
465-5747

World of Fun
613 Broad, St. Joseph
983-4954

Grand Rapids

Flippers Family Entertainment
7487 School, Jenison
457-5490

Fun Factory
Woodland Mall
940-2050

Fun Junction Cafe
5301 Northland Drive NE
363-2211

Games People Play
Eastbrook Mall
385-3221

Nickelodeon
4202 Plainfield NE
364-9525

Slots of Fun Raceway
5526 S. Division
249-3222

Strikers
303 Baldwin
457-5252

Vandy's Family Fun Center
4400 Ball Park Drive
785-0077

Holland

Bally's Aladdin's Castle
12331 James
392-4925

Fennville Amusement
301 E. Main
561-2461

Kalamazoo

Circus
Easttown
383-4170

Fun Factory
183 Westmain Mall
342-6528

Go Karts Slide-A-Way
5675 W. D Avenue
342-2405

Pocket Change
6650 S. Westnedge, Portage
323-7717

Putt-Putt Golf & Games
7206 S. Westnedge, Portage
323-0100

Tilt
5280 W. Main
384-2243

Muskegon

Laser One
232 Muskegon Mall
722-4907

Northshore Recreation
18000 Cove Avenue, Ferrysburg
846-1111

Saugatuck

Blue Star Playland
6069 Blue Star Highway
857-1044

South Haven

Fideland Fun Park
68099 County Road 388
637-3123

Craig's Cruisers Family Fun Centers

Play a round of Rocky Mountain miniature golf. Try your luck in the batting cages, or bomb around the go-cart track. You may also enjoy bumper boats, a game room, kiddie karts, and concessions. Kids, of course, love these activities.

Discounted rates are offered for groups. Craig's Cruisers has three locations: Muskegon, Holland, and Silver Lake.

Dates/Hours:	End of March–August: Daily in summer 10 A.M.–11 P.M.
Admission:	Pay by the ride
Phone:	873-2511
Address:	Call for directions

Miniature Golf

Battle Creek

Hit-Em-Here
1790 E. Columbia
965-5221

Krystalfalls Golfland
15190 Helmer Road
964-4000

Riverview Recreation
2000 E. Columbia
963-5838

Benton Harbor–St. Joseph

Captain Mike's Fun Park
10975 S. Red Arrow Highway, Bridgman
465-5747

Dave Vonk's Golf Center
3658 Niles Road, St. Joseph
429-1542

Green Acres Mini Golf
Red Arrow Highway, Watervliet
463-5731

Putters' Point
Red Arrow Highway, Bridgman
465-3198

Video Palace
5790 S. Cleveland, Stevensville
429-5748

Grand Haven

Chinook Pier Mini Golf
301 Harbor Avenue
846-2445

D&B Sports Center
18860 174th, Spring Lake
842-9878

Yogi Bear Contoured Mini Golf
10910 U.S. 31, W. Olive
847-4001

Grand Rapids

Captain's Cove
5301 Northland Drive NE
363-2211

Loeschner's Village Green
4521 Chicago Drive, Grandville
532-9124

Putt-Putt Golf & Games
5039 28th Street SE
942-9851

Strikers
303 Baldwin
457-5252

Vandy's Family Fun Park
4400 Ball Park Drive
785-0077

Holland

Blue Star Playland (Saugatuck)
6069 Blue Star Highway
857-1044

Dutchmasters
465 S. U.S. 31
392-8521

Windmill Creek Adventure Golf
631 E. Lakewood Boulevard
396-8085

Kalamazoo

Bobick's Discount Golf
6396 Gull Road
342-0381

Gold Rush Family Recreation Park
12650 N. U.S. 131
679-5385

Prospector's Ridge MiniGolf
2001 Seneca Lane
375-8200

Putt Hutt
1380 M-89, Otsego
694-4165

Putt-Putt Golf & Games
7206 S. Westnedge
323-0100

Slide A Way
5675 West D Avenue
342-5341

Muskegon

Craig's Cruisers
1551 E. Pontaluna Road
798-4936

Putters Creek
40 Causeway
744-1418

Party Packages

Your children deserve special events for special occasions, like birthdays. Some years you'll want to have parties at home, other years at sports-oriented places (like a White-caps game), parks, nature areas, zoos, and amusement centers. A glance through this book will spark plenty of ideas. Here is a sampling of party packages, and what they offer.

Chuck E. Cheese

Eastbrook Mall Grand Rapids, tel. 942-7993.
11 A.M.–10 P.M. (Saturday 11–11)
Party package $5.99 per person.
Reserved, decorated table with balloons, napkins and mats, a special party show, and a personal visit from Chuck E. Cheese. Birthday child receives 15 arcade tokens, guests each get 9. Game room and arcade for big kids; rides, shows, and climbing balls for small children. You'll need eyes in the back of your head to watch your children on a weekend; it's packed. Try for a weekday party.

Discovery Zone

4070 28th Street SE, Grand Rapids, tel. 954-9700.
Monday–Thursday 9–9, Friday–Saturday 9–10,
Sunday 11–8. Shorter hours in winter.
$3.99–$6.99 per child; discount rates for groups of
10 or more and annual passes available.
Owned by Blockbuster Entertainment, this indoor
playground and activity and fitness center caters to
2–12 year olds. Coaches supervise and encourage
children to climb and jump on the series of tubes,
tunnels, ball bins, roller slides, and an obstacle
course. Kids under 40 inches tall have their own
play area and kiddie rides. A restaurant, skill zone,
and game room are also part of "DZ."

Dome World

84th Street, just off U.S. 131, Byron Center, tel.
878-1518.
9 A.M.–11 P.M. daily. $6–$8. $6 for 3 rides or $3 per
ride, batting cage 10 balls for $.50, arcade tokens
$3 for 30. Party packages $7 per person.
Party packages include mini-golf game, bumper
boat and go-cart ride, and 10 arcade tokens for
birthday child. Free use of Dome World's heated
outdoor swimming pool. Other entertainment
includes batting cage, softball field, indoor driving
range, and playground for ages 8 and up.
Restaurant and camping available. Softball and
soccer teams play here in winter.

Kentwood Gymnastics

4525 Stauffer SE, Kentwood, tel. 281-4888.
Date/time by arrangement. Cost is $50 for up to
12 children; additional cost for additional kids.
Party package includes 1½ hours of
coach-supervised tumbling, swinging on rings and
bars, jumping on a trampoline, bouncing into
foam pits, and parachute games — all in a
gymnastics training facility. Parents bring cakes,
food, and drinks. Served in a private area. Piñatas
can be hung on men's high rings.

McDonald's Restaurant

At your local McDonald's.
Cost is $2 per child.
Standard party includes a cake, drinks, games,
favors, and a present for the birthday child. Parties
including additional food vary in price.

Putt-Putt Golf & Games

Grand Rapids: 5039 28th Street SE, tel. 942-9851
Kalamazoo: 7206 S. Westnedge, tel. 323-0100.
Winter: Sunday–Thursday 2–10, Friday 2–12,
Saturday 11–12 (arcade only).
Beginning in April: Monday–Thursday
11:30–10:30, Friday 11:30–midnight, Saturday
11–midnight, Sunday 11:30–10:30.
Party package for 6 children costs $35–$55.
Super-Fantastic and Ultimate packages are
available. Options include 1 or 2 hours of
mini-golf, 12–40 game tokens for each child, a
Saver's Club membership for golf and/or video
game tournaments. Also, birthday child gets a
tee-shirt, name on the marquee, and a photo of
partiers. Ice cream sandwiches and soft drinks
provided. A 3-day advance reservation and $10
deposit are required.

AMUSEMENT PLUS

P. J. Weber, Master Magician

P. J. Weber has made magic in 68 countries, for the last four presidents, and for Moscow's Gorbachev! A master of magic, comedy, and illusion, he customizes each routine, depending on the crowd.

He entertains at birthday and Christmas parties, school functions, company picnics, and trade shows. You may choose to have him accompanied by a purple dinosaur.

We know Mr. Weber personally, and he's good . . . really good! Not only are kids spellbound, but adults are equally enthralled.

Dates/Hours: Call to book a show
Admission: $100 for average show; commercial
             booking $550
Phone: 243-7409
Address: P.O. Box 7001, Grand Rapids 49510

Shopping Mall Events

Western Michigan's shopping malls are packed with events nearly every week, with extra-special events during seasonal holidays. Kids also enjoy special entertainment, such as sand-castle building, baseball card shows, art exhibits, and some educational expos. Call your area mall to find out what is happening and when.

Battle Creek

Lakeview Square Mall
5775 Beckley Road
979-2225

Benton Harbor–St. Joseph

Orchards Mall
1800 Pipestone Road
927-4467

Grand Rapids

Breton Village Mall
Breton Road and Burton Street SE
949-4141

Eastbrook Mall
Northeast corner of 28th Street and East Beltline
949-2550

Grand Village Mall
3501 Fairlane SW
531-5210

Green Ridge Square
Alpine at I-96
785-9455

Monroe Mall
Downtown
774-7124

North Kent Mall
4297 Plainfield NE
363-7791

Rogers Plaza
1110 28th Street SW
538-1130

Woodland Mall
Northwest corner of 28th Street and East Beltline
949-0012

Holland

Outlets of Holland
12330 James
396-1808

Westshore Mall
12331 James
393-0116

Kalamazoo

Crossroads Mall
6650 S. Westnedge
327-3500

Kalamazoo Mall
Downtown Kalamazoo
344-0795

East Towne Mall
5280 Gull Road
281-2064

Lake Center Plaza
8675 Portage Road
327-6311

Maple Hill Mall
5050 W. Main
343-4654

Southland Mall
200 Mall Drive
327-3052

Westmain Mall
West Main Street
382-4917

Muskegon

Muskegon Mall
First and Clay, downtown
722-7242

West Village Outlets
1940 Henry Street
733-5390

Shrine Circus

The Shrine Circus is an action-packed three-ring event with clowns, elephants, trapeze, motorcycle daredevils, and plenty more! Our preschoolers anxiously waited for the tigers, and were not disappointed!

The circus runs about three hours, with an intermission. Attend a matinee if your children go to bed before 10 P.M., or leave early, like we did.

Bring extra cash for concessions and souvenirs; they're expensive.

One-week stays rotate through Battle Creek (965-3308), Grand Rapids (957-1000), and Muskegon (726-2499) annually.

Dates/Hours:	11 A.M., 3 P.M., and 7 P.M. shows
Admission:	$9; discounts available
Phone:	Ticketmaster outlets
Address:	Kellogg Arena, GRCC Ford Fieldhouse, Walker Arena

AMUSEMENT PLUS

Grand Haven

Imagination Station

Ten thousand square feet of outstanding playground fun, designed by children and constructed by the community, is sure to please active kids.

Located behind the Grand Haven YMCA, Mulligan's Hollow Park also features tennis courts, basketball, a ball diamond, a grassy area, and picnic tables.

This place is spectacular — our kids call it "The Castle Park" when begging to play there.

Dates/Hours: Anytime
Admission: Free
Phone: 842-4910
Address: Off Harbor on Y-Drive, behind the YMCA

Forward Wee Roll, Inc.

A Tumblebus rolls up YOUR driveway, and the fun begins. The Tumblebus is a miniature gymnastics facility. Inside, a group of 10 to 12 children can try the vault, bars, beams, and floor under the supervision of a trained coach. Games, warm-up, and music are included.

All kids receive a sense of accomplishment.

Dates/Hours: Call to reserve the Tumblebus
Admission: $75 per hour
Phone: 669-4130

AMUSEMENT PLUS

Grand Rapids

Splash Family Water Park

Visit Greater Grand Rapids' most exciting summer fun park! The wave pool is not to be missed (swimming ability is necessary), and the water slides are worth the wait in line (hot days do draw big crowds). Our older kids especially like the water toboggan run (straight down).

The park also has an ankle-deep water activity area, lazy river, mini-golf, and sand volleyball. Concessions and a picnic area are available, as well as lockers, restrooms, and bath house.

While you must keep a close watch on the little kids, middle elementary and older kids move faster — just tell them when and where to meet you. Watch for sunburns, though. A good place for group outings and families, Splash is safe, clean, and has many lifeguards on duty.

Dates/Hours:	Memorial Day–Labor Day: 11 A.M.–8 P.M.
Admission:	Adults and older kids $13.95, ages 4–9 $10.95. After 4 P.M. $6.95
	Season passes available
Phone:	940-0400
Address:	4441 28th Street SE. East of E. Paris, north side of 28th Street

278

Grand Rapids

Vandy's Family Fun Park

Opened in summer 1994, Vandy's is fast becoming known as a great place for birthday parties and group or company outings. If you have an energetic group, play at Vandy's for a few hours, then take in a Whitecaps game — Old Kent Park is just across the street.

Vandy's boasts go-carts, mini-golf, softball and baseball batting cages, bumper boats, kiddie rides, a game room, and concessions.

Individuals may purchase activity tokens (cost varies by activity). Group packages including several activities range from $8.95 per person for 12, $7.95 per person for 25, and $6.95 per person for a group of 50 or more.

Dates/Hours: Approximately April–October, 10 A.M.–11 P.M.
Admission: No admission price; buy tokens for each activity. Group packages available.
Phone: 785-0077
Address: 4400 Ball Park Drive. U.S. 131 to West River Drive exit, across from Old Kent Park

AMUSEMENT PLUS

Grandville

Play World

Grand Village Mall's indoor playground provides loads of fun and exercise for kids. There are tunnels and slides to be explored, as well as five ball pools, foam forests, a trolley run, swing bridges, and spider nests.

Open on a drop-in basis but not a drop-off service, the playground makes a good winter or rainy-day activity when kids need to let off extra steam.

Dates/Hours:	Monday–Thursday 10–9, Friday–Saturday 10–10, Sunday 11–8
Admission:	$4.95 per child. No charge for parents or children under 1 year
Phone:	530-9222
Address:	3478 Fairlane SW, Grandville. I-96 to exit at Chicago Drive East exit; right at first light

Mattawan

Formula K Family Fun Park

Family fun includes kiddie boats and cars for preschoolers, junior racers (4–9 years), go-carts (10+ years), grand prix cars (16+ years), bumper boats, batting cages, and mini golf.

A picnic area and snack bar are located in the park. Call ahead for group discounts and birthday packages.

Dates/Hours: Spring/fall hours: 4–10;
              summer hours: 10–10
Admission: No admission charge; attractions are
              individually priced
Phone: 668-4070
Address: U.S. 131 south to I-94 west, exit 66.
              Turn left off exit ramp and watch for sign

AMUSEMENT PLUS

Muskegon

Michigan's Adventure Amusement and Wild Water Park

Muskegon is the home of Michigan's largest amusement and water park, boasting 20 great thrill rides, 11 water slides, a lazy river, wave pool, children's activity pool, shows, games, and food.

Michigan Adventure Park has the only three roller coasters in the state!

Dates/Hours: Weekends beginning second weekend in May; then mid-June–Labor Day

Admission: $15 per person; 2 and under free
Coupons and special discounts available

Phone: 766-3377

Address: Eight miles north off U.S. 31 from Muskegon's Russell Road exit, 4750 Whitehall Road

Muskegon

Pleasure Island Water Park

Ask any 10 year old at Pleasure Island: the "Black Hole" slide DOES live up to its billing! Other thrilling water rides include The Twister and Thunder Falls.

A family-oriented water park, Pleasure Island has twin speed slides, two corkscrew slides, paddle boats, bumper boats, kiddie slides and play areas (both water and land), mini-golf, and water cannons. Concessions and picnic areas are located within the park.

Dates/Hours: End of May through Labor Day weekend: 10:30 A.M.–8:30 P.M.

Admission: All day $14.95; under 48 inches tall $10.95; after 4 P.M. $8.95 per person

Phone: 798-7857

Address: From I-96, exit west of U.S. 31 on Pontaluna Road, 1½ miles to 99 E. Pontaluna Road

ACTIVE SPORTS

Gus Macker 3-on-3 Basketball Tournaments

Gus Macker headquarters in Belding challenges players with the world's largest 3-on-3 basketball tournament. It's great fun for spectators, too!

Gus Macker manages tournaments in 65 cities throughout the U.S. Southwestern Michigan Macker tournaments are played in Battle Creek (May), Belding (July), Grand Rapids (May's Charity Jam), and Kalamazoo (August) during the summer months.

The tournament is open to children over age 6, with special adult divisions for over-40 and senior citizens.

One hundred thousand spectators attended the Kalamazoo Macker in 1993's tournament. The other Mackers draw similar crowds!

Dates/Hours: Register 30 days prior to your chosen tournament
Admission: Enter as a 4-person team, $80 per team per tournament
Phone: 794-1500, or 1-800-876-4667 (leave message) Macker headquarters: 121 E. Main Street, Belding 48809

Basketball

ACTIVE SPORTS

287

Optimist Club Tri-Star
Basketball Contest

Your 8–13 year old can pass, dribble, and shoot his or her way to the Optimist Club's District Championships in this mid-March Tri-Star Basketball Contest. Register at the event.

The contest is held in many cities and towns; call your local Optimist Club for details.

Dates/Hours: Mid-March Saturday, registration at
12:30 P.M.
Admission: Free
Phone: 375-2013, Kalamazoo
Address: Call for location

Belmont

Cannonsburg Challenge Mountain-Biking Weekends

Whether you have competitive or leisurely mountain bikers in the family, the Cannonsburg Challenge Weekends have biking courses for you. On Saturday, choose between a running/biking biathlon, family road tours, Cannonsburg's marked trail ride, competitive slalom, and 3.5-mile challenge courses.

Sunday's events include cross-country, slalom, and kids' races. Various age brackets and all skill levels are represented. The races draw 50–100 riders for each event, and over 2,000 spectators for the weekend.

Each biker needs an approved helmet and bike. Some races have separate kids' divisions and participant awards for all. Don't miss the prize drawings!

Dates/Hours:	Usually a mid-April weekend, and third weekend in October
Admission:	Kids races and family fun tours, $5; competitive races $10–$20
Phone:	453-4245
Address:	6800 Cannonsburg Road. U.S. 131 to West River Drive, becomes Cannonsburg Road at East Beltline

Biking

ACTIVE SPORTS

Grand Haven

Grand Coast 50 Bicycle Tour

On the Sunday before Memorial Day, join 50 families or more for the Grand Coast 50, a beautiful 50-kilometer bicycle tour (that's 35 miles).

Beginning at Harborfront Place in Grand Haven, tour riders travel along the Grand River on quiet roads toward Grand Rapids, then loop back to Grand Haven.

All ages may participate — even 6 year olds have ridden on this tour!

Dates/Hours:	Sunday before Memorial Day
Admission:	$11 includes lunch; register in advance
Phone:	Rock & Road Cycle, Grand Haven: 846-2800
Address:	Begins and ends at Harborfront Place, Grand Haven

Biking

ACTIVE SPORTS

Hart-Montague Trail

In Michigan, 44 abandoned railroad beds have been converted into fantastic biking trails. They are also great for hiking and cross-country skiing.

The Hart-Montague Trail runs just west of Manistee National Forest, and offers a variety of terrain and postcard scenery. The 22.5-mile paved trail passes farms and cherry orchards, a special treat during blossom time in May and the brilliant color-changes in fall.

Climb the White River Lighthouse Museum tower when you get to Montague — it offers a wide-angle view of Lake Michigan and the dunes. It's hard to imagine a nicer family outing!

A shuttle service picks bikers up at various points along the trail, but call first to make sure it's running (schedule and phone number are posted at trail heads). Bike rentals are available in Montague (893-2453) or Mears (873-4271).

Dates/Hours:	Daylight hours
Admission:	Per person: $2/day, $10/year
	Families: $5/day, $25/year
Phone:	873-3083
Address:	Call for directions to trail entries

Biking

ACTIVE SPORTS

Grand Haven/Holland

Lakeshore Drive Trail

Lakeshore Drive has a beautiful 24-mile paved bike path running from Grand Haven to Holland. Try roller blading or walking part of its length.

Dates/Hours: Anytime
Admission: Free
Address: Along Lakeshore Drive

ACTIVE SPORTS

Grand Rapids

Kent Trails

Starting just south of John Ball Park, Kent Trails (a former Penn Central Railroad line) connects three beautiful parks — Douglas Walker Park in Byron Center, Johnson Park in Grandville, and John Ball Park in northwest Grand Rapids.

Take the 15-mile route to Douglas Walker Park if your children are older (it's 15 miles back, too!); they'll love the covered railroad bridge. This trail ends in front of the Byron Family Restaurant, usually coincidental with a hearty appetite; or bike the extra three miles to the park and enjoy your own picnic.

The seven-mile route from John Ball Park to Johnson Park will suit younger kids' short legs better. Both routes are marked with aqua-colored signs, and run through a variety of urban and rural settings.

Dates/Hours: Daylight hours
Admission: Free

Kalamazoo/South Haven

Kal-Haven Trail

The Kal-Haven Trail has grown in popularity every year, with increased use by hikers, horseback riders, skiers, and snowmobilers.

This 34-mile crushed limestone trail combines stunning natural beauty with small towns and modern conveniences. Ride past streams, lakes, wetlands, forests, blueberry farms, and vineyards between Kalamazoo and South Haven.

The South Haven trailhead is located on Blue Star Highway at the Black River just northeast of South Haven. The Kalamazoo trailhead is ¾ mile west of U.S. 131 on 10th Street between G and H Avenues. Intermediate parking areas are located at Kibbie, Bloomingdale, Gobles, and Kendall.

Dates/Hours:	Daylight year-round
Admission:	$2.50
Phone:	Van Buren State Park: 637-4984 or 637-2788

Biking

ACTIVE SPORTS

Kalamazoo/South Haven

Kal-Haven Trail Blazer

Choose your route from a 25, 40, 60, or 100-mile bicycle tour on measured roads and the highly popular Kal-Haven Trail. Nine hundred cyclers participate in the largest one-day event of its kind.

Children under 12 must be supervised by an adult.

Call for information about the shuttle service for those who pre-register for the tour. You may end in either Kalamazoo or South Haven.

Dates/Hours:	Second Saturday in mid-May
Admission:	Pre-registration: $11/person, $25/family
	At event: $13/person, $30/family
Phone:	657-3232
Address:	Begins at Kalamazoo Central High School, 2432 N. Drake Road

Biking

ACTIVE SPORTS

Rockford/Belmont/Wayland

Mountain Bike Trails

Pando and Cannonsburg Ski Areas have marked mountain bike trails that are open all summer for the thrill seekers in the family. A challenging 13-mile trail at Yankee Springs Recreational Area near Gun Lake also has shorter loops.

Be sure to wear insect repellent — the trails wind through dense woods and can be very buggy. A helmet is also a must: low-hanging branches and emerging roots over the trail make it a bumpy ride.

Dates/Hours: Daylight hours anytime
Admission: Free
Address: **Pando:** U.S. 131 to West River Drive; north on East Beltline to Belding Road; 7 miles to 8076 Belding Road

Cannonsburg: 6800 Cannonsburg Road. U.S. 131 to West River Drive, becomes Cannonsburg Road at East Beltline in Belmont

Yankee Springs: U.S. 131 to Wayland exit, follow signs to Recreation Area

Biking

ACTIVE SPORTS

296

Rockford

Pando Challenge Mountain Bike Races

The three Pando Challenges have races and tours for riders of all ages and abilities. Noncompetitive family tours, downhill slalom, biathlons, cross-country races, and 5k runs are on the schedule. State championships are held during an October event.

Kids' races have two divisions: 6 and under and 7–12. All racers receive medals and are entered in prize drawings. Cross-country races have 17-and-under divisions; otherwise they are divided by male/female and skill levels. Participants need an approved helmet, bicycle, and lap-counting ability.

This mountain-biking series is one of the largest in the Midwest, averaging 700 riders and 2,000 spectators for each weekend. The event includes food, prize drawings, and games.

Dates/Hours:	Weekends at end of May, mid-July, and early October. 9 A.M. registration
Admission:	Varies by race. $5–$15 advance registration
Phone:	453-4245
Address:	U.S. 131 to West River Drive, north on East Beltline/Northland to Belding Road, 7 miles to 8076 Belding Road

According to the West Michigan Bowling Proprietors Association, most bowling centers offer Sportschildren's bumper bowling (no gutter balls!), and many have birthday packages and group excursion rates. The following bowling centers offer bumper bowling and/or special children's programs; for those not listed, check your local telephone book.

Battle Creek

Ken Nottke's Bowl
775 W. Columbia
963-9121

M-66 Bowl
19794 M-66
962-9597

Marshall Lanes, Inc.
1154 W. Michigan, Marshall
781-3125

Springlake Lanes
245 E. Roosevelt
965-3241

Benton Harbor–St. Joseph

Blossom Lanes
23-5 M-139
927-3174

Coloma Lanes
6025 Mountain, Coloma
468-7127

Kelley's Bowl
2705 Cleveland
983-3034

Lakes Bowl
Sister Lakes
944-1208

Lakeshore Lanes
6201 Red Arrow Highway, Stevensville
429-5421

Wil-O-Paw Lanes
4890 Paw Paw Lake Road, Coloma
468-4601

Grand Haven

Idle Hour Lanes
213 W. Savidge, Spring Lake
842-1358

Northshore Recreation
1800 Cove Avenue, Ferrysburg
846-1111

Starlite Lanes
1305 S. Beacon Boulevard
846-2820

ACTIVE SPORTS

Westland Lanes
6790 S. Harvey, Spring Lake
798-4508

Grand Rapids

Eastbrook Lanes
3550 Lake Eastbrook Boulevard SE
949-7650

Fanatorium Recreation
40 Jefferson SE
454-7914

Holiday Bowling Lanes
609 28th Street SW
532-5077

Michigan Lanes Bowling
1503 Michigan NE
459-4551

Rockford Lanes
117 E. Bridge, Rockford
866-0200

Westgate Bowl
4486 S. Alpine NW
784-6450

Holland

Century Lanes
478 E. 16th
392-7086

Holland Bowling Center
215 Central Avenue
392-1425

Northland Lanes
308 N. River
392-7146

Zeeland Lanes
541 E. Washington Avenue, Zeeland
772-2322

Kalamazoo

Continental Lanes
3645 Vanrick Drive
343-2626

Eastland Bowl of Kalamazoo
5570 Gull Road, Comstock
382-4077

Harpo's Lanes
4500 Stadium Drive
375-1378

Holiday Lanes
2747 S. 11th
375-6100

Lake Shore Lanes
301 N. Richardson
649-0203

Pine Grove Lanes
M-40 north, Gobles
628-2161

Plainwell Lanes
515 N. 10th, Plainwell
685-5878

Rainbow Lanes
Red Arrow Highway west, Paw Paw
657-4870

Richland Lanes
9900 E. D Avenue, Richland
629-9388

Sunset Lanes Bowling Center
8336 Shaver Road, Portage
327-7061

Templins Sunset Lanes
504 Western Avenue/M-40 north, Allegan
673-2671

Wayside Lanes
3330 Stadium Drive
375-2550

Muskegon

AMF Muskegon Lanes
1150 Whitehall Road
744-2451

Bob Hi Lanes
2930 S. Getty
733-1928

Brunswick Lanes
441 W. Western Avenue
722-3489

Fraternal Order of Eagles
621 W. Western Avenue
726-5117

Fremont Lanes South
5885 S. Warner, Fremont
924-6730

Muskegon Lanes
1150 Whitehall Road, North Muskegon
744-2451

Northway Lanes & Billiards
1751 Evanston Avenue
773-9181

Pin Crest Lanes
6571 Airline Road, Fruitport
865-3215

Ravenna Bowl
2915 S. Slocum Road, Ravenna
853-2275

Bowling

ACTIVE SPORTS

Sherman Bowling Center
1531 W. Sherman Boulevard
755-1258

Westland Lanes
6790 S. Harvey
798-4508

White Lake Bowling Lanes
115 S. Lake, Whitehall
894-4103

Canoe Trips

Floating down a river in a canoe allows views of nature and wildlife that you might not otherwise see: turtles, blue herons, and deer, for example, are regularly spotted along West Michigan riverbanks.

Because canoe trips can take a couple of hours, you might want to bring snacks along with you. Be sure to bring bug repellent too, but leave home anything that you don't want to get wet! The following organizations offer canoe rentals:

AA Canoes
7994 E. Kilgore, Kalamazoo
342-1913

AAA Rogue River Canoe
12 E. Bridge, Rockford
866-9264

Areawide Canoe Raft & Tube
25 E. Water, Newaygo
652-6743

B & B International
1609 Seminole, Kalamazoo
349-9939

Chinook Camping
5471 W. 112th, Grant
834-7505

Canoeing

ACTIVE SPORTS

Croton Dam Float Trips
5355 Croton Drive, Newaygo
652-6037

Double R Ranch
4424 White Bridge Road, Belding
794-0520

Grand Rogue Camp & Canoes
6400 West River Drive NE, Belmont
361-1053

Happy Mohawk Canoe Livery
735 E. Fruitvale Road, Montague
894-4209

Indian Valley Camp & Canoe
8200 108th SE, Middleville
891-8579

Kellogg's Canoes
250 W. Michigan, Hesperia
854-1415

Lumbertown Canoes & Kayak
276 Ottawa, Muskegon
728-2276

Mendon Country Inn
440 W. Main, Mendon
496-8132

Old Allegan Canoe Rental
2722 Old Allegan, Fennville
561-5481

Paw Paw River Campground
5355 M-140, Watervliet
463-5454

White River Campground
E. Fruitvale Road, Montague
894-4209

Wilderness Ridge Campground
5256 130th Avenue, Hamilton
751-5684

Annual Free Fishing Weekend

For two days in June, the Michigan Department of Natural Resources encourages experienced fishermen (and -women) to introduce children, friends, or family members to the joys of fishing. No fishing license or trout-salmon stamp is required, although all of the other regulations are still in force.

Fish on the Great Lakes or inland lakes, rivers or streams. Watch your littlest angler reel in the biggest catch!

For good fishing spots, contact your local tackle shop or the Michigan DNR (517) 373-1280. The Future Fisherman Foundation offers children's workbooks and materials for first-timers: call (708) 381-9490.

Dates/Hours: Two days in June
Admission: Free, except for bait

Fishing

ACTIVE SPORTS

Grand Rapids

Pathways to Fishing

This special sport show clinic helps kids learn the elements of fishing. The clinic includes 12 stations of hands-on basics, taught by experts; it is sponsored by the Grand Rapids chapter of the Michigan Steelheaders.

The Rubbermaid/BASS Casting Kids Contest has also become part of the sports show, with state finals held on Sunday, the last day of the show.

All ages are invited to catch a fish in the "Twin Trout Ponds," with proceeds to benefit Harper Creek Optimist Club's children's causes.

Dates/Hours: March weekend. Part of sport RV show
Admission: Free for children who color and bring
               sport show page from *Grand Rapids Press*
Phone: 530-1919
Address: Grand Center, downtown Grand Rapids

Lowell

Kid's Golf Camp

Held at Deer Run Golf Course, the Kid's Golf Camp gets children, beginning at 8 years old, started in golf — the sport that looks so easy, but can be sooooooo hard.

One-week sessions are offered 8 A.M.–12 NOON daily. It's the best way to learn the game: all at once!

Dates/Hours: June–August
Admission: $125–$150
Phone: 897-8481
Address: I-96 to Cascade Road, Lowell

North Muskegon

Family Golf

This challenging par 3 golf course and driving range located in North Muskegon has watered fairways, practice putting and chipping facilities, and club and cart rentals. Excellent for family golfing fun!

Western Michigan is blessed with many, many public golf courses and driving ranges, and some offer excellent junior golf programs, complete with lessons, club rentals, and course time. Call your nearby course.

Dates/Hours: Set a tee time
Admission: 9 holes, $3.50
Phone: 766-2217
Address: 4200 Whitehall Road, North Muskegon

Grand Rapids Amateur Hockey Association
285-4600
Youth hockey leagues, Learn to Skate (ages 4–17),
then Learn to Play classes. October–April. Learn to
Skate $150, Team $400 for 23 weeks of play.

Hockey Development Programs
349-1246 (Kalamazoo)
Hockey school for kids at various levels. Three
1-week camps held in August.

Kentwood Hockey and Skating Association
455-KHSA
Hockey and figure-skating programs, camps.

Kalamazoo Optimist Hockey Association
349-7825 or 342-9836
Learn to Skate program: beginning to advanced clubs
and classes. Hockey competition takes place at Wings
Stadium and Lawson Arena.

Kalamazoo Wings Hockey Club
349-9772
The K-Wings, a team of excellent 16–20-year-old
players, belongs to the North American Junior
Hockey League. The team plays 30 games per season,
home games at Wings Stadium. October–mid-March,
tickets $4.

Horseback Riding

Flying Horses Ranch

S. Yankee Springs Road, Middleville, tel. 795-7119.
Horseback riding in Yankee Springs Recreation
Area. Ride without a guide. Horsedrawn hayrides.
April–October, $13/person, $25 for two. Group
rates available.

Huntington Valley

7878 N. 43rd, Augusta, tel. 731-2500.

Kentree Equestrian Park

4861 Michigan, Ada, tel. 949-1430.
Tuesday–Friday 9 A.M.–7 P.M., Saturday–Sunday 9–5.
Riding academy with full-service boarding.
Programs, arena, group lessons.

Northland Farms

3625 4 Mile Road, Grand Rapids, tel. 363-7970.
English and dressage, indoor arena, boarding,
training. Private $25; semi-private $18; group $15.
Horse sales.

Royal Q Stables

North on U.S. 131 to Stanwood, near Canadian Lakes on Buchanan Road, tel. 972-2090. 15-minute rides available for $5, 1 hour $13, 2 hours $23. Ponies for children under 6. Hayrides/sleighrides anytime in season ($25 deposit, $5/person). Barnyard petting zoo includes peacocks! Open 7 days a week year-round.

Spring Valley Training Center

78th Avenue, Lawton, tel. 423-6141.

Stonehill Stables

5770 Alaska Avenue, Alto, tel. 868-6692. Riding lessons. Call for class schedule.

Triple Challenge Farm

9404 100th SE, Caledonia, tel. 891-0333. Tuesday–Saturday 9–5. World-class farm offers horseback-riding lessons.

West Michigan Equestrian Center

2100 Riley Thompson Road, Muskegon, tel. 766-3879
Riding lessons, varying rates. Dressage or hunt. Open all year.

Ice-Skating

Michigan's winters are loads of fun if you get into the winter groove. Ice-skating has many variations, and is good exercise! Your recreation department will have information about outdoor rinks. Following are western Michigan's indoor ice-skating rinks.

Battle Creek

The Rink

> 75 Houston Street, downtown, tel. 962-4076. September–May open skate, ice hockey, rental, skating lessons, figure skating, hockey league.

Grand Rapids

Belknap Ice Arena

> 235-9940
> 30 Coldbrook NE. Just east of Plainfield, south off Leonard to Division, east on Coldbrook. Fee to skate; rentals available. Open skating available for the whole family. Parent-tot skating class. High school and league hockey team play.

Cascade Ice Arena

Patterson Avenue, between Burton and 28th
Streets. Scheduled to open late 1994-1995.
Recreational, speed and figure skating, and ice
hockey.

Kentwood Ice Arena

6178 Campus Park SE, Kentwood, tel. 698-0100.
East Kentwood High School at Kalamazoo Avenue
and 60th Street SE. Open skate and recreational
activity.

Kalamazoo:

Lawson Ice Arena

Western Michigan University, Howard Street, just
north of Stadium Drive, tel. 387-3050.
Open skate and open hockey.

Wings Stadium

3600 Van Rick Drive, tel. 345-1125.
Open skate (admission $2.50, rental $1).

Muskegon:

L. C. Walker Arena

Off U.S. 31 at 4th and Western in Muskegon, tel.
726-2939.
October–mid-March: hockey, figure skating,
rentals. Public skate Saturday–Sunday 2–4.

Muskegon

Luge — Speed on Ice!

The Muskegon Winter Sports Complex is home to the Midwest's only luge track. Also included are lighted cross-country ski trails, an ice-skating rink, and a sports lodge. Weather, however, is not guaranteed.

Prospective lugers (age 8 and over recommended) can test out this exciting sport — helmets, sleds, and coaching are available. No excuses — there is a beginner's run, and it's safe and well-supervised!

Spectators are invited to attend luge competitions, held almost every January or February weekend, or check out the annual Media Luge Challenge, held at the end of January.

Olympian Mark Grimmette, who took fourth place in Lillehammer, began his luging career at the Muskegon luge track.

Dates/Hours:	After January 1, public hours are Friday–Sunday 3–10
Admission:	Beginner luge track: adults $12; 17 and under $8 (includes helmet, sled, coaching)
Phone:	744-9629
Address:	Muskegon State Park, 3560 Memorial Drive, North Muskegon

Roller Skating

Battle Creek

Little Wheels
242 Hamblin
965-0871

Midway Roller Rink
11448 E. Michigan
965-7117 or 965-7427

Benton Harbor–St. Joseph

ARK Skating
453 Highland, Benton Harbor
925-3247

Lakeshore Roller World
5567 Red Arrow Highway, Stevensville
429-7700

Ramona Roller Rink
93127 County Road 690, Dowagiac
424-5736

Grand Haven

Grand Haven Roller Rink
219 N. 7th
842-5910

Grand Rapids

Bloomfield Gardens Roller Rink
28 17 Mile Road NE, Cedar Springs
696-1483

Byron Rollercade
3651 84th SW, Byron Center
878-3515

Kentwood Roller Skating
14 52nd Street SE, Kentwood
534-8106

Plainfield Skating Center
1655 4 Mile Road NE, Grand Rapids
364-7900

Roll Away Bowling & Skating
805 E. Main, Lowell
897-0001

Tarry Hall Roller Skating
3330 Fairlanes, SW, Grandville
534-8235

Woodland Sport Center
2100 28th Street SE, Grand Rapids
452-8623

Holland

Grand Roller Rink
12521 James Street
399-3081

Kalamazoo

Great Skate Roller Rink
10496 Portage Road
327-8006

Maple Park Skating Center
1506 N. Main, Three Rivers
279-2710

Roller World
7491 Stadium Drive, Kalamazoo
382-4600

Roller World
76 10th, Plainwell
685-2020

The Rink
4525 Long Lake Drive, Portage
327-0407

Muskegon

Rollarena
1775 Evanston Avenue
773-5538

Roller Fox
12189 E. Apple Avenue, Ravenna
853-2971

Run for Your Life!

Runners, walkers, and joggers have plenty of outlets for their competitive urges in western Michigan. Races are held every month, some with special kids' divisions, and some that are just for fun.

Pietro's Fun Fasta Eat Pasta 5k Run, held in Grand Rapids in April, has become one of THE races for kids, with six divisions — including a Diaper Derby. Call 452-3228 for information.

The Old Kent River Bank Run, held in Grand Rapids in May, is the largest 25k race in the nation, attracting runners from all over the map.

Call the Gazelle Sports Race Information Hotline at 1-800-879-2626 for information about upcoming races in the West Michigan area, or pick up a complete Events Calendar from Gazelle Sports, located in Grand Rapids, Holland, and Kalamazoo.

Sailing Lessons

Experience the wind in your hair, the freshwater spray on your face, and sometimes an "Uh oh . . . I think we have a problem." Learn to sail the right way, with lessons!

Grand Haven

> Grand River Yacht Club
> 846-4032

Grand Rapids

> Reeds Lake Yacht Club
> 949-1750

Holland

> Macatawa Bay Yacht Club
> 335-5815

Muskegon

> Torresen Sailing School
> 759-8596

Saugatuck

> Tower Marina
> 857-2151

Cross-Country Skiing

These locations offer outstanding cross-country skiing. Also, be sure to check out the parks and the state parks in "The Great Outdoors." Call your local/county recreation department for trails near you.

Berrien Center

Love Creek County Park
471-2617
6 marked, groomed trails, 10 km. All levels. Night skiing.

Cassopolis

Dr. T. K. Lawless Park
476-2730
7 marked, groomed trails, 6 km. All levels. Night skiing.

Fred Russ Forest Park
445-8611
3 marked, groomed trails, 6 km. Beginner to intermediate.

Ionia

Bertha Brock Park
527-0478
3 marked trails, 13 km. Beginner to intermediate.

Skiing

ACTIVE SPORTS

Kirk Park
846-8117
2 marked trails, 3 km. Beginner to intermediate.

Pigeon Creek
846-8117
2 marked trails, 3 km. Beginner to intermediate.

Grand Rapids

Kent Trails
Access points: Johnson, John Ball, and Douglas
Walker Parks, and Byron Center's 84th Street Parking Area. 15-mile wooded trail, beginner to intermediate.

Kent County Airport Trails
Thornapple River Drive, south of I-96
2 miles open fields, beginner.

Lamoreaux Park Trail
$\frac{1}{8}$ mile north of Bailey Park Drive on Coit Avenue
5-mile wooded trail along Grand River, beginner.

Palmer Park Trail
Kaufman Golf Course, Clyde Park between 44th
and 52nd, Wyoming. Monday–Saturday 9–7, Sunday 10–6; Trail fee $1 per person.
5 miles wooded/groomed trails. Beginner to intermediate.
Ski rentals available, smallest size toddler size 10.
Clubhouse has hot chocolate, coffee, and snacks.

Skiing

ACTIVE SPORTS

Provin Trails Park
4 Mile Road and Bird Avenue. Parking on 4 Mile Road.
2-mile wooded trail. Beginner to expert.

Robinettes
361-5567, northeast corner of 4 Mile and East Beltline.
Ski the orchards, or connect with Provin Trails
Rentals available in two-hour blocks.

Seidman Park Trail
Honey Creek Avenue between 2 Mile Road and Conservation
6-mile wooded trail. Intermediate to advanced.

Wahlfield Park Trail
M-37 and 8 Mile Road. Park on M-37.
3-mile wooded trail along Mill Creek. Intermediate.

Pando Ski Center
874-8343
3 marked, groomed trails, 8 km. All levels.

Kalamazoo

Bittersweet Ski Resort
694-2820 or 694-2032
2 marked, groomed trails, 6 km. All levels. Night skiing, food.

Celery Flats Interpretive Center
329-4522

Skiing

ACTIVE SPORTS

S. Westnedge, go two miles south of I-94 exit, east to Garden Lane

Kalamazoo Nature Center
381-1574
7000 N. Westnedge

Kal-Haven Trail State Park
637-2788
South Haven to Kalamazoo
1 groomed trail, 54 km. beginner.

Prairie View Park
383-8778
1 marked, groomed trail, 5 km. beginner.

Mears

Hart-Montague Trail
873-3083
1 marked trail, 35 km. All levels. Night skiing, food.

Muskegon

Hoffmaster State Park
798-3711
4 marked trails, 10 km. All levels.

Muskegon State Park
744-9629
2 marked, groomed trails, 8 km. All levels. Night skiing.

Middleville

Yankee Springs Recreation Area
795-9081
4 marked, groomed trails, 16 km. Advanced.

Niles

Madeline Bertrand Country Park
683-8280
4 marked, groomed trails, 6 km. Beginner to intermediate. Night skiing, food.

Sawyer

Warren Dunes State Park
426-4013
1 marked trail, 10 km. Beginner. Food.

Skiing

ACTIVE SPORTS

Downhill Skiing

Bittersweet, Otsego

600 River Road, Otsego (US 131 to exit 49B), then M-89 west. Left on Jefferson Road to River Road. Bittersweet on the left. Tel. 694-2032. Weekdays 10 A.M.–10:30 P.M., Weekends/holidays 9 A.M.–10:30 P.M. Call for lift-ticket information.

16 runs: 5 on rope tows, 4 other beginner, 4 intermediate, 3 difficult. One double, 4 triple chairlifts. 300-foot vertical drop. Sparks program for ages 4 and up. Ski school for all levels. Complete snow making and grooming, food service.

Cannonsburg Ski Area

6800 Cannonsburg Road, Grand Rapids, tel. 874-6711. Weekdays 10–10, Weekends 9 A.M.–10 P.M., late November–mid-March. Lift tickets $12–$20. Rentals $5–$10.

23 runs, every level. Programs for small children; Mighty Mites Program (4–12 year olds) includes skiing from 9 A.M.–3 P.M., hot chocolate breaks and lunch. Cost for series of 6 is $175 (or $35 each). Private lessons: $70 for series of 3 lessons. Free skiing for kids under 6 years.

Mulligan's Hollow

Grand Haven. Located on Harbor Drive behind the Grand Haven YMCA, tel. 874-7051. Monday–Wednesday and Friday 5–9, Thursday 5–8, Saturday 1–9, Sunday 1–6. Lift tickets: Parents ski free, pay only for kids. YMCA members $7. Weekday/weekend $10. Weekend snowboarding $12. Season passes available.

328

8 beginner and intermediate runs, 3 rope tows. 150-foot vertical drop. Snow-making capability; night skiing. Three 1-hour lessons $20. Lighted ice rink and warming house with concession stand.

Pando Ski Center

8076 Belding Road, Rockford, tel. 873-8343 or 453-4245. Monday–Friday 5–10 P.M., Saturday–Sunday 10 A.M.–8 P.M. Lift tickets: Monday–Friday $8, Saturday–Sunday $12. Rental $12, under 6 $6, snowboard $15. Lessons: private $15.

No waiting in long lift-lines on seven well-groomed slopes, served by five rope tows. 125-foot vertical drop. Ski school available every day for downhill and cross-country skiers.

Swiss Valley Ski Area

Jones. US 131 south to M-60 (at Three Rivers, south of Kalamazoo), west to M-40, north to Swiss Valley, tel. 244-5635. Weekdays 10–10, Saturday 9 A.M.–10 P.M., Sunday 9 A.M.–10 P.M. Lift tickets: vary from $10 to $20, depending on the day of the week and number of hours.

11 runs, 225-foot vertical drop, 3 chair lifts, 4 rope tows. Snow making, grooming. Ski school, race programs, special discounts. Fun races $.50 per run. "Mushroom Patch": Weekends/holiday instruction for ages 3–9. Includes lunch, lift, rental, and lessons, 9 A.M.–3 P.M.

Timber Ridge

626 Maple Hill Drive, Kalamazoo. US 131, exit 44 (D Avenue) north of Kalamazoo. West to 23½ Street, turn

right. Timber Ridge on the left, tel. 1-800-253-2938. Hours: Weekdays 10–10, Saturday 9 A.M.–10 P.M., Sunday 9 A.M.–8 P.M. Lift tickets: Vary from $8 to $20, depending on day of the week and number of hours. Under 6 ski free. Rentals $8–$14.

15 runs, 240-foot vertical drop, variety of lifts. Ski-school rates: classes $7, privates $18. Free lessons for first-timers 8 years and older. Polar Cubs: complete weekend program for 8–12 year-olds (3½-hour lesson, lunch, hot chocolate). Race events. Field trips as school functions get special rates.

Sledding and Tobogganing*

Greater Grand Rapids

Big Apple Run

Manhattan Recreation Center, East Grand Rapids. Fulton to Cascade Road, east to Manhattan Road, south to Center. There are some bumps, and the hill is fast and steep. A secondary hill in the area has a gentler slope.

Bruiser Hill

North on DeHoop Avenue from 28th Street. The park is on the west side of the street. Great for the older kids to go fast, but hang on tight — there is a 45-degree angle! The hill offers a gentler slope to the south and a "rump burner" to the north. A challenging walk up.

Charlie's Dump

Georgetown Township Soccer Bowl, Jenison. Rosewood at 20th Avenue, Jenison. Unique hill with four sides that empty onto a soccer field. Portable lights and a dumpster. No trees.

Creston Christian School

East side of Diamond at Leonard NE, Grand Rapids, northeast side, is a favorite with a long, gentle slope. A nearby playground offers a diversion for youngsters.

*thanks to *Advance* for hills listings

Sledding

ACTIVE SPORTS

I-96 Speedway

I-96 near Muskegon, exit 16, first access road to the right. Steep, professionally designed sledding hill with lights.

Johnson Park Hill

I-196 to 28th Street SW, Grand Rapids. Just west of intersection (where 28th Street becomes Wilson Road). Long, sloping hill with small hill off to one side. Difficult climb for toddlers. No night lights.

Tree Trek Slopes

Richmond Park. At the intersection of Richmond Street and Powers Avenue on Grand west side. Top-notch sledding because of lighting and steps to one side of the slope. The two tough runs through the woods are not for beginners. There is also a long, gently sloping hill.

Sledding

ACTIVE SPORTS

Swimming

Whether your kids are into serious workouts or serious goofing off, swimming is excellent exercise for them and for YOU! Open swims or family swims are scheduled at community pools, YMCAs, and private pools.

Every child should know how to swim and be comfortable around the water. Get your kids into swimming lessons early!

If your child wants to swim competitively, there are many well-run age-group swim teams in the West Michigan area. The season usually runs from fall through the winter with daily practices and Saturday meets. Call your local recreation department to find the age-group swim team nearest you.

Dates/Hours: Pool hours vary by season
Admission: Free or small charge

ACTIVE SPORTS

Kentwood

Indoor Triathlon

Kentwood Recreation Department hosts a one-day indoor triathlon for kids 8 and older and adults. Participate in running, biking, and swimming events. It's a great way to get in some winter exercise!

Dates/Hours: Usually third Saturday in January
Admission: Residents $10; nonresidents $15
Phone: 531-2391
Address: East Kentwood High School, Kalamazoo and 60th Avenues

Play It Again Sports

Recycle your kids' outgrown sports equipment, and suit up for next year at this franchised resale sporting goods store.

The stores are located in Grand Rapids (241-2550, 530-9779), Holland (399-9906), Kalamazoo (345-9119), and Muskegon (733-6490).

Dates/Hours: Monday–Friday 10–9, Saturday 9–6
Admission: Cost of any purchases
Address: Call for information

Athletic Clubs

Many western Michigan athletic clubs have children's programs to encourage active movement and fitness. Grouped by ages, classes are offered in swimming, tumbling, tennis, basketball, racquetball, and aerobics. Available to members and nonmembers, some clubs have weekly try-a-little-of-everything sessions, too.

Schedule your child's birthday party at an athletic club. Supervision and a full range of activities are included. Prices vary, and you must book them in advance.

ACTIVE SPORTS

Recreation Department Activities

Call your local recreation department for its current offering of sports activities and lessons. Swimming, bowling, soccer, gymnastics, tennis, golf, and more are available!

YMCA

The YMCA has facilities in five western Michigan cities: Battle Creek, Grand Haven, Grand Rapids, Kalamazoo, and Portage.

Family and kids' activities vary by facility. Some of the possibilities are a swimming pool, gymnasium, exercise rooms, racquetball and tennis courts, whirlpool and sauna.

The Y is a safe and fun environment for kids — for burning off energy, learning or improving skills, and making friends.

Phone for information: Battle Creek (962-7511), Grand Haven (842-7051), Grand Rapids (458-1141), Kalamazoo (345-9622), and Portage (324-9622).

Facilities

ACTIVE SPORTS

SPECTATOR SPORTS

Grand Rapids

Walter Mitty Motors Mini Grand Prix

Held annually, the Walter Mitty Motors Mini Grand Prix sports mini race cars with 5-horsepower engines and fiberglass bodies. The race is run around the Radisson Hotel in downtown Grand Rapids. The event benefits the Arthritis Foundation.

Dates/Hours: Third Saturday in September, opening
              ceremonies at noon
Admission: Free
Phone: 361-7746
Address: Downtown Grand Rapids

Grattan

National Enduro and National Sprint Grand Prix Races

Motorcycle and go-cart racers run on two-mile road courses to accumulate points in a competition against corporate teams. Auto races are two-day events at Grattan Raceway near Belding.

Vintage autos and motorcycles are often shown.

Dates/Hours: Weekly; call for details
Admission: $5 general admission
Phone: 691-7221
Address: U.S. 131 north of Grand Rapids to 10 Mile. East 12 miles to Lessiter, then right 1 mile

Battle Creek

Stan Musial World Series

Battle Creek is a baseball kind of town, and the people here love their tournaments!

The Stan Musial World Series, a Battle Creek fixture for over 25 years, is a championship tournament for the Double ABC League; these guys are really good! Former professionals and ex-college ballplayers from the nine national regions (including Puerto Rico) play for the crown.

Held Thursday–Monday during the third and fourth weekends in August, the tournament draws 1,000-2,500 spectators for each game.

Big Ten Baseball Championships and NCAA Division III Baseball Championships are also played at the stadium in Battle Creek.

Dates/Hours: Third and fourth weekends in August
Admission: $5 per game
Phone: 962-2240, or City Parks and Recreation
              Department (966-3431)
Address: C. O. Brown Stadium, Bailey Park

343

Detroit Tigers Alumni Grand Slam

Played for the benefit of the Children's Miracle Network, this doubleheader pits "old" Tiger greats against members of the community (who each donate $500 for this opportunity).

A West Michigan Whitecaps game follows the doubleheader at Old Kent Park.

Dates/Hours: August, watch for announcement of specific date
Admission: Approximately $6
Phone: 776-2000
Address: 4500 West River Drive. U.S. 131 to West River Drive, north of Grand Rapids

344

Grand Rapids

West Michigan Whitecaps

Professional minor league baseball (class A) is a big hit in southwestern Michigan. The West Michigan Whitecaps host 70 of their 140 games at the newly constructed Old Kent Park. Capacity is 6,900, split between box, reserved, and lawn seating.

Families will especially enjoy the ballgames and many kid-pleasing extras — including entertainment, giveaways, and fireworks.

Call the Whitecaps office to schedule a birthday party or pre-game picnic. Groups of 20 or more may arrange discounted tickets, preferred seating, and some other nice perks. Availability is limited; call early for your group outing.

Bring ball gloves — foul balls are fair keepers!

Dates/Hours:	Weeknights: April–May 6:35 P.M., June–August 7 P.M. Weekends: 2 P.M. Check schedule
Admission:	Box tickets, $6. Reserved $4.50. Lawn seating $3. Undated tickets (20 or more) $4
Phone:	Your area Ticketmaster office, or 1-800-CAPS WIN
Address:	4500 West River Drive. Take U.S. 131 to West River Drive exit, just north of Grand Rapids

CBA's Grand Rapids Mackers

In a few short years, the Mackers, formerly named the Hoops, have become perennial playoff contenders with a loyal western Michigan following. The Mackers are one of the nation's winningest CBA teams, and several of its players have gone on to the NBA ranks.

Half-time entertainment rates a thumbs-up, too!

Dates/Hours:	2-3 games per week, late November–March. Start times 7:05 P.M. or 7:35 P.M.
Admission:	$7–$13.50. Season tickets are available, as are blocks for large groups
Phone:	456-3333
Address:	Welsh Arena, downtown Grand Rapids

Grand Rapids

Grand Rapids Press High School Basketball Tournament

Area high school teams vie for this hotly contested championship during Christmas break each year. This is a great activity for basketball fans of all ages!

Dates/Hours: Watch the *Grand Rapids Press* for specific schedules

Admission: $3

Phone: 771-3990

Address: Grand Rapids Community College Ford Fieldhouse, 111 Lyon NE, downtown

College Sports — Men and Women

Junior high and high school kids will easily be able to check out western Michigan's college-level play in their favorite sports! For schedules and ticket prices, contact college athletic departments:

Aquinas College
Information line
459-8281 x3120
Main sports office
459-8281 x3101

Calvin College
Athletic office
957-6046

Grand Valley State University
Sports office
895-3275

Grand Rapids Community College
Athletic office
771-3990

Hope College
Sports hotline
394-7888
Athletic tickets
394-7691

Kalamazoo College
Sports hotline
337-7347
Sports information
337-7303

Kalamazoo Valley Community College
Athletics
372-5395

Western Michigan University
Athletic ticket office
387-3092

Grand Rapids

Holiday Jam — Gymnastics at Its Best

Beam, bars, floor, and vault . . . double backs, sukes, and summis. Gutsy, hard-working girls perform astounding gymnastics tricks and routines at the Holiday Jam.

A showcase of local and national talent, the Holiday Jam features more than 500 girls, all ages, competing at levels 4–10 and Elite. The Olympic team is selected from the Elite ranks.

Future stars ages five and up will especially enjoy this three-day event. Call Kentwood Gymnastics to find out when each level performs.

Dates/Hours:	Second weekend in December, Friday–Sunday 8 A.M.–10 P.M.
Admission:	Adults $5/day, kids 12 and under $3 Adult weekend pass $7.50; kids $5
Phone:	281-4888
Address:	Grand Rapids Community College Ford Fieldhouse, downtown

Kalamazoo

Kalamazoo Wings Hockey

There are two reasons to attend a Wings ice hockey game: either you like hockey, or you want a change of winter's pace. Either way, these games are reasonably priced, and filled with good hockey (the team goes to the playoffs most years).

The Kalamazoo Wings are the IHL farm club for the National Hockey League's Dallas Stars, and many Wings players have been called up to the Stars. Kalamazoo is one of the last smaller cities to support a team in the prestigious International Hockey League.

Eighty-two games are played in a regular season, with 41 at home. Playoffs can add an extra month to the season.

Dates/Hours: October–May (including playoffs)
Admission: Regular season $8–$9
Phone: 345-5101
Address: Wings Stadium: Sprinkle Road, just
            south off I-94

351

Muskegon Fury Ice Hockey

The Muskegon Fury is a professional franchise of the Colonial Hockey League.

The management wants families to attend games, and offers special promotions to heighten kids' enjoyment of ice hockey. Fan Appreciation Night is a big hit, as is Beach Night (fans get to go out on the ice!).

Crowds average 2,500-3,000 spectators per game.

Dates/Hours:	October–March
Admission:	$6–$8. Student and senior discounts available
Phone:	726-2400 or 726-5058
Address:	L. C. Walker Arena: Off U.S. 31 at 4th and Western

Muskegon

Muskegon Race Course

Kids can get up close to the fence to watch harness racing at the Muskegon Race Course. Just one of two harness race tracks in Michigan, the Muskegon Race Course is conveniently located near U.S. 31 just outside of Muskegon.

Horses run rain or shine. Group rates and buffet dinners are available.

Dates/Hours: April–October, Friday–Saturday 7 P.M.,
               Sunday 5 P.M. Also Thursday in
               July–August
Admission: Clubhouse $3.50, grandstand $2.50
               Children 12 and under free
Phone: 798-7123
Address: U.S. 31 to Airline Road exit, just off the
               freeway

353

Grand Rapids

Michigan Open Speed Skating Championship

At Grand Rapids' Belknap Arena, over 50 Olympic-caliber speed skaters compete in four different events: 500, 1000, 1500, and 3000-meter races. This Open Regional Championship is sponsored by the Grand West Michigan Speed Skating Club.

Children of all ages, including 6 and under, are also invited to try this demanding sport. Contact the Speed Skating Club's Bill Weaver (887-9693) for information. Skaters work out three times weekly.

Dates/Hours:	Second weekend in December, Saturday 10–5 and Sunday 9–1. Date subject to change
Admission:	Free
Phone:	456-3694
Address:	US 131 to Leonard exit, south on Division, east on Coldbrook. Just east of Plainfield

Kalamazoo

Professional Ice-Skating Shows

Held at Kalamazoo's Wings Stadium (345-5101), Muskegon's Walker Arena (726-2400), and Battle Creek's Kellogg Arena (965-3308), three professional ice-skating shows alternate tour routes each year. Dates vary; watch for announcements.

Ice Capades: Now owned by Olympic champion Dorothy Hamill. Skaters act out stories, such as Cinderella. $10–$18.

Disney on Ice: Owned by Ringling Brothers, who contract for use of Disney characters.

America Tour Ice Show: All performers have won Olympic or World medals. This group skates solos and "ensembles." Adults $20.50 and $28.50. Kids ages 2–12 $18.50. Under 2 free, sitting on parent's lap.

Kalamazoo

Skate the Zoo

Western Michigan University is the annual host for Skate the Zoo, a midwestern figure skating competition. Endorsed by the Ice Skating Institute of America, the three-day competition attracts over 300 competitors ages five through adult.

We recommend that you see the freestyle competitions; creative choreography really comes into play! Call for times.

Dates/Hours: Mid-April weekend, Friday 12–6,
Saturday–Sunday 9–6
Admission: Free
Phone: 387-3050
Address: Lawson Ice Arena: Stadium Drive to
Howard, on WMU's campus

Grand Haven

Great Lakes All-American Sport Stunt Kite Competition

In an all-day event sponsored by the Mackinaw Kite Company, competitors fly specially constructed sport kites to synchronized music.

All levels of competition are represented. Kite-flying lessons and demos are provided, as well as opportunities to fly manufacturers' sport kites.

The whole thing takes place on the beach. It's great for families!

Dates/Hours: Weekend before Memorial Day
Admission: Spectators free (after admittance to state park); competitors $60
Phone: 846-7501
Address: Grand Haven State Park

357

Grattan

Motorcyclist Association Championship Cup Series Final Race

A variety of production motorcycles to grand prix style racers run the Championship Series Final Race on an early October weekend at Grattan Raceway's asphalt track (located near Belding).

The Motorcyclist Association's largest event is the Vintage Bike Race, held the third weekend in May.

Dates/Hours: October (call to confirm date)
Admission: Adults $15; 12 and under $3
Phone: 691-7221
Address: U.S. 131 north of Grand Rapids, exit 10 Mile. East 12 miles to Lessiter, then right for 1 mile

Sparta

Annual Klein Rodeo

Sanctioned events fill this three-day rodeo, in which more than 180 contestants compete in six events.

Events include bull riding, bareback riding, calf roping, and steer wrestling. There's even some bullfighting! The rodeo draws 3,500 adults and children each day.

Campgrounds are available.

Dates/Hours:	Labor Day weekend 2 P.M.
Admission:	Adults $9; children 8–12 $3; under 8 free
Phone:	887-9945
Address:	Corner of Alpine Avenue (M-37) and 13 Mile Road, Sparta

SPECTATOR SPORTS

Skiing

Michigan Show Ski Championships

Cypress Gardens comes to western Michigan when six to eight water-ski show teams compete in this annual tournament. Each team skis a one-hour show, with pyramids, dance lines, and barefoot skiing. Judges award points for performances — they are fabulous!

Teams come from all over Michigan and northern Indiana for these championships. A good family outing could begin at Coldbrook Park, combining picnicking with top-notch athletics. The beach and swimming are closed for the day.

The competition is sponsored by the Kalamazoo County Parks Department, which also organizes several other park events, including Boogie on the Beach and the nationally ranked Mid-American Sport Kite Classic. Call for information.

Dates/Hours:	9 A.M.–finish, last Saturday in July
Admission:	$3 per carload
Phone:	383-8778
Address:	Coldbrook Park: I-94 east of Kalamazoo to exit 85, south 1 mile, follow signs to park

Kalamazoo

USTA Boys 18 and 16 National Tennis Championships

Many current and past tennis greats have provided championship-level tennis entertainment at the Boys 18 and 16 National Championships, held at Kalamazoo College's Stowe Stadium for many years. Age divisions are 18 and under and 16 and under, singles and doubles.

This event is a "must" for aspiring college and pro players, and Kalamazoo does a fine job of hosting the tournament. Aspiring tennis players will really be revved up after a day or two at the National Championships!

The championships open with a Sunday exhibition match, leading up to the doubles finals Thursday and Friday evenings, and singles finals on the following Sunday. This is truly exciting tennis!

Dates/Hours:	Second week in August
Admission:	Advance or at the gate: adults $5; children under 17 $3
Phone:	337-7343 or 337-7344
Address:	U.S. 131 to Stadium Drive east, just before downtown Kalamazoo, left on Academy

CAR TRAVEL
SURVIVAL GUIDE

Man Alive! What a Drive!

We're sure YOU'VE never heard "Are we there yet?" or "How much farther?"

But WE have, and we offer these activities and games to make the miles move faster.

Besides taking along an enormous sense of humor, pack a box of fun and handy items. You'll wonder how you traveled even one mile without your survival kit. This kit shortens airplane trips, too.

- Travel version of your favorite game (our kids love Trivial Pursuit cards and Tot Trivia)
- Deck of playing cards
- Pads of paper with stiff cardboard backs, pens and pencils
- Cassette tapes for headphones or car stereo
- Books and crossword puzzles (only if your travelers aren't prone to carsickness)
- Kleenexes, wet wipes, plastic bags
- Snacks — apples, oranges, grapes, animal crackers, fruit snacks (less messy than soda crackers and chips)
- A jug of something to drink and paper cups

Make Me Laugh, I Dare You!!

One child is "IT," and the others invent a phrase for him. Try "the dog's ear," or anything wacky!

"IT" must answer every question others ask him with that phrase, and NOT LAUGH.

The other players might ask him, for example, what he wants for his birthday, or what he brushes his teeth with, or what instrument he would love to learn to play.

The player who makes him laugh is "IT" for the next round.

In Grandmother's Attic

In grandmother's attic you might find all kinds of wonderful, weird and wacky things.

"In my grandmother's attic," begins the first player, "I found . . ."

What she found, when the game is given the wildest scope, may be anything beginning with the letter *A* — say, an anteater.

Player number two repeats the introduction plus the first player's article, and adds her own, beginning with *B*. So the game goes around, alphabetically, with each player repeating the growing list and adding a new item.

Players are out if they can't repeat the list correctly.

To add variety to the game, limit the category. For instance, in grandmother's attic there are only food items or books!

The License Plate Game

There are lots of games you can play using the letters and numbers from the license plates on passing cars. Below are a few game ideas:

- Make a list of all the states spotted on the license plates. The player who finds the most wins!
- Choose a word, say, the name of the place you are traveling to. Have everyone spell it out with the letters found on license plates. Of course, the letters must be found in the proper order.
- Players can also collect numbers. Start with the number 1, and find it on a license plate; then 2, 3, 4, and so on. This becomes more difficult after double figures are reached.
- Try to spot all the letters of the alphabet in order just by using license plates.

Back-Seat B-Ball

One person makes a basket with his or her arms and the other players shoot baskets with wadded pieces of paper. Points are scored for each basket. But points are deducted for any foul balls that leave the court and go into the front seat!

The responses "yes" and "no" cannot be used in conversation for 15 minutes.

The fun begins when everyone tries to trick the other players while at the same time avoiding saying "yes" or "no" themselves!

Using a piece of paper and pencil, each person creates two coupons that describe two nice things the creator will do for someone else on the trip. For example, "I, Maranda, promise to open the door for my mother every time she wants to get out of the car on this trip."

This is an old one but a good one!

Someone thinks of an object and gives one hint: whether it is an animal, vegetable or a mineral.

The players ask 20 questions phrased to be answered with a "yes" or "no."

A guess at the object counts as a question.

Keep track of questions — ONLY 20!!

CAR TRAVEL SURVIVAL GUIDE

Geography

Ask the players to write down as many of the United States and/or Canadian provinces and territories they can think of.

Players can also name the state capitals. Get a list from an encyclopedia, your local library, or a map if you can't remember them all. One player names the state, the other responds with the capital.

Give them the name of a state and ask them to name all the others that border it.

Higher, Lower

The leader picks a number between 1 and 1000 but tells no one.

Each player in turn tries to guess the number.

The leader can only respond by answering "higher" if the guess is larger than the number, or "lower" if the guess is smaller. The player who finally guesses the number becomes the next leader.

Lottery Winner

Players take turns pretending that they've won a million dollars and describing how they will spend the money.

Hum a Tune

Each person takes a turn humming a tune and the other
  players try to guess the tune's title.
The category of the tune can be announced each round.
  (Try movie themes, top-forty tunes, or commercials.)

CAR TRAVEL SURVIVAL GUIDE

376

Marshmallow Sculpture

Put 20 or 30 marshmallows in a shallow box along with several small boxes of raisins and a box of toothpicks. Players create sculptures of people, places, and things using the ingredients.

I Saw That

In TEN WORDS or less, players takes turns describing a movie or a television show that everyone has seen.

The other players try to guess the title.

Receive 1 point for each correct guess. The player to get 10 points first wins.

Where's Your Next Stop?
What Will You See?

One player asks "Where's your next stop?"

Another player must answer by choosing a word that begins with *A* — perhaps "Alaska."

"What will you see?" Answer with another *A* word, such as "airplane."

The next time, ask the same questions with the letter *B*. For another challenge, see how fast you can go.

What Time Is It?

On long trips, restless riders often ask the time. In this game, no one can ask the time.

Every so often, though, a leader who is the only one who can see the watch, can ask the others, "What time is it?"

The player closest to the correct time gets 1 point. Five points wins the game.

Buzz

One player chooses a number between 1 and 9 — for example, 6. That's the buzz number.

Start counting around the circle of players — but each time the buzz number comes up — by itself or part of a larger number (6, 16, 63, 426) replace the number by the word "Buzz."

You are out if you say the number instead of buzz!

A more advanced way to play is with multiples of the buzz number. For example, if 6 is the buzz number, 12, 18, 24, and 30 must be replaced with the word "buzz."

Simon Says

Simon says, "Put your hands on your head." Simon says, "Suck your thumb."

But if Simon doesn't say it — DON'T DO IT — or you are OUT! The last one in is "Simon" for the next round.

Terrible Tongue Twister

Repeat after me: BIG FAT HEN
BIG FAT HEN, COUPLE OF DUCKS
BIG FAT HEN, COUPLE OF DUCKS, THREE BROWN
BEARS . . .
This one becomes funnier and funnier as the repeater tries
to build on and repeat this complicated tongue twister
all the way to . . . TEN TUMBLING TODDLERS TUM-
BLING AND TRIPPING OVER TEN TRILLION TOYS!

Big Fat Hen
Couple of Ducks
Three Brown Bears
Four Running Hares
Five Funky Females
Six Simple Simons Sitting on a Stone
Seven Sicilian Sailors Sailing the Seven Seas
Eight Egotistical Idiots Echoing Egotistical Ecstasies
Nine Napping Gnomes Nipping and Napping at Knat
Knuckles and Nectarines
Ten Tumbling Toddlers Tumbling and Tripping over Ten
Trillion Toys

CAR TRAVEL SURVIVAL GUIDE

CONVENTION &
VISITORS BUREAUS

Southwestern Michigan Tourist Council
2300 Pipestone Road
Benton Harbor, MI 49022
(616) 925-6301

Battle Creek Area Visitor & Convention Bureau
34 W. Jackson Street
Suite 4-B
Battle Creek, MI 49017
(616) 962-2240

Grand Haven–Spring Lake CVB
One S. Harbor Drive
Grand Haven, MI 49417
(616) 842-4499

Grand Rapids Area CVB
140 Monroe Center, NW
Suite 300
Grand Rapids, MI 49503
(616) 459-8287
1-800-678-9859

Holland Area CVB
171 Lincoln Avenue
Holland, MI 49423
(616) 396-4221

Kalamazoo County CVB
128 N. Kalamazoo Mall
P.O. Box 1169
Kalamazoo, MI 49007
(616) 381-4003

Muskegon County CVB
349 W. Webster
Muskegon, MI 49440
(616) 722-3751
1-800-235-FUNN

Saugatuck-Douglas CVB
P.O. Box 28
Saugatuck, MI 49453
(616) 857-1701

CHAMBERS OF COMMERCE

Allegan
(616) 673-2479

Cedar Springs
(616) 696-3260

Coloma
(616) 468-3377

Colon
(517) 278-5985

Dowagiac
(616) 782-8212

Fremont
(616) 924-0770

Grand Haven-Spring Lake
(616) 842-4910

Grandville
(616) 531-8890

Greenville
(616) 754-5697

Hastings
(616) 945-2454

Holland
(616) 392-2389

Ionia
(616) 527-2560

Marshall
(616) 781-5163

Montague
(616) 893-4585

Otsego
(616) 694-6880

Paw Paw
(616) 657-5395

Pentwater
(616) 869-4150

Plainwell
(616) 685-8877

Rockford
(616) 866-2000

South Haven
(616) 637-5171

Sparta
(616) 887-2454

Wayland
(616) 792-2265

Whitehall
(616) 893-4585

Zeeland
(616) 772-2494

Index

391